"KICK is one of the most in ministries working with youn story thus far has been prc wholeheartedly believe that the years ahead will be even more so. Joe Lowther is an outstanding leader and I am not only inspired by the story of KICK but by his example too."
Gavin Calver, Director of the Evangelical Alliance

"Joe's leadership at KICK has demonstrated that the Good News of Jesus Christ is the most significant message for young people. The book is filled with inspirational stories rooted in a firm theological foundation. What an incredibly uplifting read!"
Graham Daniels, General Director of Christians in Sport

"Great organisations like KICK have a powerful impact on evangelism."
**Archbishop Justin Welby,
The Archbishop of Canterbury**

"Having met Joe Lowther at the start of his KICK journey, I am honoured to endorse his book, KICK and his commendable journey. Joe compellingly illustrates the transformative power of combining sports with spiritual guidance through the story of KICK and its journey, providing an educational and inspiring narrative filled with personal anecdotes and the ministry's milestones. This book is a must-read for anyone involved in youth work, sports ministry, or community service, as it exemplifies the remarkable achievements possible when faith is put into action."
Rev. Warren Evans, CEO of Sports Chaplaincy

"We tragically all know young people who are overwhelmed by hopelessness. This book is living proof that there is a better story. The many case studies and testimonies from KICK's journey will inspire anyone passionate about the emerging generation that change is possible, hope is coming and joy can be experienced in the present."
Ruth Jackson, Presenter at Premier Radio

"If the Church is going to reach this generation of young people, we will need vision, faith and action. At the heart of KICK's Story is vision, mission and risk; it recounts a challenging and inspirational journey. What an opportunity for the Church to reach young people in its community! Keep going Joe and team!"
Rev. Les Issacs OBE, Founder of Street Pastors

"I am so fascinated and grateful to God for my esteemed friend, Joe Lowther, his life and the work of KICK. In a world filled with distractions and uncertainties, it's rare to find a beacon of light that not only guides but transforms lives. In this book, my dear friend embarks on a journey that transcends the boundaries of conventional wisdom and delves into the profound impact of sport intertwined with the power of faith. As you delve into the pages of this book, prepare to be inspired, challenged and uplifted. Whether you're a sponsor, church leader, church and youth organisation, a parent, a mentor, or simply someone who believes in the extraordinary potential of our youth, this book will resonate deeply with you. It is a testament to the profound truth that in every sport, love and compassion, there lies an opportunity to sow seeds of love, faith and hope that can truly change the world."
Pastor Rasaq Ibrahim, RCCG UK

"There are only a few things in my life that stir my passion and inspire more hope than sport. One of those things is the Gospel. What I appreciate most about this wonderful book is the fervent emphasis on both of these things, and that even with Joe Lowther's love of sport, it is the good news of Jesus that has truly captivated his heart. Moreover, it is that great story that is the engine room of this remarkable journey of favour, growth and impact. KICK's Story is packed full of astonishing stories of God's faithfulness and blessing and you cannot help but be inspired by what is possible when a Godly movement of people implement a game-changing vision. This story will bring profound encouragement and insight to all who read it. Joe is the real deal and I am so proud of my friend for writing this brilliant book."

Phil Knox, Evangelism and Missiology Specialist at the Evangelical Alliance

"KICK is an incredible organisation, and it has an incredible story! Joe tells the story of KICK's phenomenal growth and impact intertwining Biblical reflections, leadership lessons and stories from the frontline. This book is a powerful reminder that God is at work and that He cares about young people!"

Andy and Jo Frost, Share Jesus International

"Joe is an exceptional pioneer who trusts God for his every step, as he recounts the stories of KICK's early years. The pages within give testimony to the faithfulness of God and the obedience of all involved. KICK is now a major player within the youth work scene. Prayer and obedience has fuelled its growth."

Neil O'Boyle, National Director of British Youth for Christ

"Joe is a passionate advocate for young people; an experienced leader championing the Gospel and its relevance for younger generations. Through this combination, he has gleaned wisdom that should be heeded."
James Fawcett, Church of England

"This book is full of principles, applications and God's faithfulness. I have watched Joe and KICK grow through the years. What a journey, what a read and what a God."
Yan Nichols, Director of YWAM UK

"KICK and Joe Lowther are the real deal. At a time when the UK church's engagement with young people has tragically plummeted, KICK have bucked that trend. With an inspirational story of God's call, white-hot faith and dependence on God in prayer and the leading of the Spirit, this book releases hope that God hasn't finished His saving and transforming work in our younger generations. This is a deeply encouraging and challenging book that reveals what God can do when a group of people are willing to live all-in for Jesus. As I read it, I felt the Spirit saying, 'Whom shall I send?' The only response can be, 'Lord, here I am. Send me.' Read it and let it fuel the fire in your heart for all God has called you to do for His glory."
Rev. Canon John McGinley, Leader of the Myriad Church Planting Programme

"Here is a story worth telling — of how a vision to reach young lives became reality. Packed with accounts of wonderful personal transformation, this book should carry a contagious faith warning!"
Kate Patterson, Gift of Blessing Trust Director

"At a time when young people face such huge challenges, I'm so thankful for the way that God is raising up KICK to bring his love and compassion to a generation who need to know he's there for them. Joe Lowther is a thoughtful humble leader whom God is so clearly using to build a team bringing help and hope to young people across the nation."

**Tim Morfin OBE, Founder & Chief Executive,
Transforming Lives for Good (TLG)**

At KICK, their commitment to 'transforming lives' isn't just a tagline; it's a daily reality they live out. This book tracks the origin and growth story of an organisation on the frontline of making a difference whilst offering biblical illustrations that empower us all to get involved in God's mission. Joe Lowther's inspiring journey of personal obedience and commitment to following a call driven by his passion for education and sport is remarkable. Yet, he does not position himself as the hero of this story; God is. The book addresses the pressing need to reach young people in innovative ways, meeting them at the point of need where they spend most of their formative years. As the narrative unfolds, it becomes evident that KICK's mission extends beyond just provision of outstanding services; it's about building relationships, fostering hope, and creating a supportive environment where young people can flourish. You cannot help but be inspired by the adventure! KICK's Story not only motivates us to focus on the next generation but urges us to embrace bold leaps of faith and pursue mission with unwavering dedication in our own lives too."

Dave Boden, Executive Director of Grace Foundation

"When I think of Joe, three words come to mind all beginning with the letter 'P'. Joe is Passionate, Pioneering and Persistent... He is passionate about personally walking with Jesus and living a life that glorifies Jesus and points people to Jesus: particularly young people whom Joe is passionate about serving inside and outside the four walls of the church. His work with KICK aligns with his passion for reaching a generation that could be said has not yet connected with Jesus and His Church. Joe is a relentlessly pioneering character, which is clear through watching his work at KICK and all the new ground they have taken as an organisation, across the nation. He is also persistent in his pursuit of reaching young people with the Gospel in creative and innovative ways. Joe is great and I am sure his book will be a blessing to all and any who read it."

Zeke Rink, Dreaming The Impossible (DTI) Youth Network Associate Pastor, Vineyard

KICK STORY

A WILD RIDE OF CALLING, ADVENTURES AND A GLORIOUS GOD

Copyright © 2024 Joe Lowther

The moral right of the author has been asserted.

Apart from any fair dealing for the purposes of research or private study, or criticism or review, as permitted under Copyright, Design and Patents Act 1998, this publication may only be reproduced, stored or transmitted, in any form or by any means, with prior permission in writing of the publishers, or in any case of the reprographic reproduction in accordance with the terms of licences issued by the Copyright Licensing Agency. Enquiries concerning reproduction outside these terms should be sent to the publishers.

PublishU Ltd

www.PublishU.com

Scripture from the Holy Bible, New International Version®, NIV®. Copyright © 1973, 1978, 1984, 2011 by Biblica, Inc.™ Used by permission of Zondervan. All rights reserved worldwide.

All rights of this publication are reserved.

Thanks

To Laura, the boys and the KICK family.

I want to thank Matt King, who approached me, pursued me and has backed me over my time at KICK. He is a visionary and inspirational person to work with. I want to thank all of the trustees, past and present, who have been like Marvel's Avengers, bringing their superpowered skills and erudite insights for the benefit of KICK and the blessing of young people. I want to thank Tom Rutter for being brave to become our founding coach and giving two decades of his career to KICK. To Trevor Patterson, Jonn Burns, Barry Mason and all those at British Youth for Christ for conceptualising and launching KICK. For everyone at Holy Trinity Church Richmond for being so welcoming to all who have served at KICK and for housing our HQ for over twenty years.

For the three hundred and eight staff members who have worked for KICK during our history, with notable mentions to Mark Anderson, Jo Bradbury, Hans Sims, Andy Dutton, Becci Lee, Jonathan Sanders, Rachel Hollings, Simon James, Jonny Wright and Simon Gee, amongst others who have given years of sacrificial service in leadership roles. For other sports ministries, partners, schools and churches who have worked shoulder to shoulder with KICK during this time. Thank you to all the KICK Academy volunteers who have delivered sports ministry faithfully to young people at weekends and evenings in their own time. To those who have generously given financially, such as personal donors, grant-making trusts and funders. For the advice and guidance of various people over the years, particularly my coach, Peter Ptashko, and mentor, Michael Graham. For all those who have prayed for KICK and any I have missed unintentionally: Thank you.

Personally, I want to thank my wife, Laura Lowther, who has been a constant supply of wisdom, support and love. There are many occasions where you have given sage counsel on tough decisions and I couldn't have helped run KICK without you. I want to thank you and the boys for bearing with me as I have written this book and for keeping me sane with laughter and your patience. Thank you to James and Naomi Lowther, my parents, who have always believed in me. Your encouragement has enabled me to scale mountains. Thank you too to my wider family for your love, support and encouragement. Thank you to all those at my church, at Christian Fellowship in Richmond, who have taught so many of the principles that I have tried to apply over these years at KICK. I want to thank all the contributors to the book – your testimonies have warmed my soul, and I pray they will bless others. I want to thank my astute editors for the patience, investment, challenge and reassurance to shape this book: thank you Holly Price, Phil Knox, Jonathan Souray and Alison Souray. I want to thank Matt Bird for the structure of his book writing course and for all those who have endorsed the book. Finally, I want to thank God for His hand on my life and His work at KICK. I hope this book brings glory to Him and is a place of worship and thanksgiving for all He has done.

Many thanks to all those from KICK (past and present) who wrote their story for KICK:

Adam Charlton, Alastair Park, Alex Mclean, Andrew Dowey, Andy Dutton, Becks Louis, Becci Lee, Cliff Underhey, Davey Murphy, Hans Sims, Jack Newman, James Lowther, Jo Bradbury, Joe Mallett, Jonathan Sanders, Jonny Wright, Kate Patterson, Louise Corless, Mark Anderson, Matt King, Mike Wakeham, Peter Brooks, Peter Debrah Mensah, Penny Cox, Rachel Hollings, Rob Curtis, Samuel Braga Tavares, Simon Gee, Simon James, Stuart Kennett, Tom Rutter, Zoe Cross.

Contents

Introduction – KICK-Off

PART ONE
| MISSION |

Chapter 1: Mission; KICK's Story

Chapter 2: Mission; Spiritual Application

PART TWO
| ASPIRATION |

Chapter 3: Aspiration; KICK's Story

Chapter 4: Aspiration; Spiritual Application

PART THREE
| COMPASSION |

Chapter 5: Compassion; KICK's Story

Chapter 6: Compassion; Spiritual Application

PART FOUR
| EXCELLENCE |

Chapter 7: Excellence; KICK's Story

Chapter 8: Excellence; Spiritual Application

PART FIVE
| INTENTION |

Chapter 9: Intention; KICK's Story

Chapter 10: Intention; Spiritual Application

PART SIX
| INTEGRITY |

Chapter 11: Integrity; KICK's Story

Chapter 12: Integrity; Spiritual Application

Conclusion

Epilogue – The Way Forward

Introduction
KICK-Off

Are you passionate about the next generation? Do you dare to believe in God and desire to make a difference? KICK's Story will aim to share insights of faith and testimonies of hope and celebrate God's generous provision. Questions you might ask yourself, such as "Is there any point in reaching this generation?" or "Why don't we just move on and invest in the following generation?" can spring to mind. Such questions were posed to me by a friend who'd lost hope with the drop off in church attendance, the resistance to established ways of engaging with Christianity for young people, and the stark contrast in passionate engagement in many issues other than God. Do you identify with feeling lost about engaging young people? Do you sense hope rise when you see the passion of youth engagement in important matters of environment, social justice and inclusion? This book will aim to shed light on examples of where and how God is working in the lives of children and young people. Join us on a wild ride of calling and adventure, to marvel at a glorious God.

1. Wild Ride of Calling

My head was spinning. I had handed in my notice at City Gateway, the school where I was principal and had served for nine years. Only God, the CEO and I knew in the organisation. I felt like He was calling me out for over a year. He was so gentle, but I could sense it. I resisted. I had worked hard and was proud of what we'd achieved to go from five to two hundred and fifty staff. It was a demanding environment, and I often did not feel like I had time to think within it. I'd closed my ears and resisted His voice. My wife Laura had sensed it earlier (as always) and warned me that we faced being outside God's will. I wrestled with this but had my head in the sand. Then, one icy December, God spoke to me plainly three times in consecutive days from the book of Isaiah that He was calling me to move on. The game was up. I knew it was time to resign. I was scared, but I knew it was better to be in His will than outside of it. I met with the CEO the next day and resigned, giving them nine months to replace me, as I knew Ofsted was looming and I wanted to end well.

So, here at Easter 2014, the clock was ticking on being without a job and with two small children. I sat down on Good Friday to watch the Passion of Christ, the movie, as any former film student might do, to get me in the mood for reflecting on what Jesus went through at the Cross. I know it embellishes the Biblical story, but it always gets me in the zone to be grateful to Him. As I did, I reflected on what I'd heard about this organisation, based in Richmond, called KICK. They did sport, education and mission. I thought, "I love sport; I'm trained in education and I blimming love mission." I wondered if they might have some jobs going. Maybe I should enquire, I thought. No, it's Good Friday, Bank Holiday weekend and better to contact them next Tuesday. So, I settled back to watch the film and halfway through, I got up to grab a drinks break. As I did, I checked my emails, and the Chair of KICK, Matt King, had emailed me?! He said, "Our Director has just resigned to go and become a Vicar and we have met to pray about closing down the organisation." As they had prayed, they had been challenged by Judges 6:36–40 about casting out a fleece. My name had come up and would I ever consider leaving my job as headteacher to come and run KICK? Incredible. I wrote back, "I was about to email you... and you've emailed me!"

So, we started a process, but not before Ofsted decided to come to our school in May on my birthday. They brought with them five inspectors across four days for an intense inspection. As any headteacher would be, I was nervous about an Ofsted Inspection. If we'd failed our inspection, I would doubtless have lost my job in ignominy. However, instead, we achieved an Outstanding Grade in every single area of the Common Inspection Framework. The Lead Inspector told us he had never given an overall outstanding grade in his career of twenty years. Our staff were brilliant and demonstrated their values-driven competency, but I also knew that God had blessed us. I was grateful to God for honouring us as a team in this way. Rather than losing my job, I was able to end well, starting at KICK in the following November 2014. I turned up for work on my first day, but there was no one to greet me. I couldn't get into the office for two hours. When I did, there were boxes all over the place, and there was no WIFI and no heating for the first and coldest three months of the year. But I knew it was exactly where God had called me to be. I never looked back and was excited about what God would do. His ways are higher than our ways.

I arrived at KICK with a background in education, a love for sport and, most importantly, a passion for mission. KICK's mission is to transform young people's lives with

God's love through sport and support. At the time of writing this book, KICK interacts with more than twenty-eight thousand young people in seven regions of the UK and has over ninety staff.

2. Missional Adventure

KICK's mission is to transform young people's lives with God's love, through sport and support. Young people express a sense of hopelessness: one-third of 16–24 year olds in the UK report evidenced depression or anxiety.[1] According to the NHS (2023) since Lockdown, "Rates of a probable mental disorder rose from one in ten in 2017 to one in six." Young people are anxious but they are also unhappy – one in five young people now self-harm[2] and concerningly sixty percent of terrorism referrals are for under twenty year olds.[3] Many young people experience a sense of hopelessness. Therefore, our solution is to go into schools to deliver professional services of PE National Curriculum, Transformational Street Dance provision, Solutions Focused Mentoring and Schools-Based Chaplaincy. We then look to equip local volunteers, from local churches to reach local young people through coaching in sport or dance at the weekend called KICK Academies. KICK Academies provide a vital stepping stone for young people to be welcomed out of school and into church. We want to provide an opportunity for young people to experience both sport and faith at the weekends. We want to be 4D in our approach to Demonstrate of God's love in schools; Declare the Gospel through our church-based KICK Academies; to help young people make a Decision about who Jesus is for them; so that if they would like to they

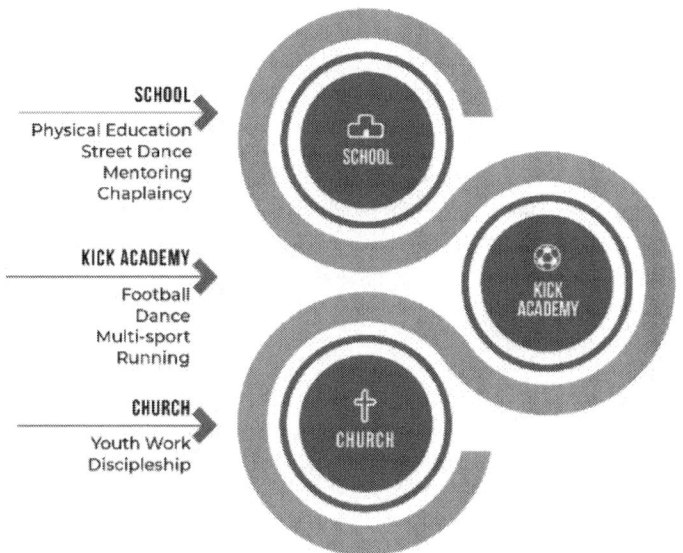

can be Discipled by local churches for a lifetime.

So, we have developed a sustainable, scalable and successful model for the mission. The model is sustainable as it is largely funded via government funding for school provision, and by training volunteers for the KICK Academies, there are no ongoing costs to churches. The provision has been successful as it has grown in the last eight years. We have progressed from engaging two thousand five hundred to twenty-eight thousand young people per week. At the time of writing, our staff team has dramatically grown from seven to ninety-two employees, with sixty volunteers. We now deliver over forty different Sports and Dance disciplines. Our Mentoring provision has grown from twenty-two learners in 2015 to one thousand two hundred and sixty-one per week today. In July last summer, we saw one hundred and one young people give their lives to the Lord. Finally, our approach is scalable. There is a school and a church in every community in the UK. KICK sits in between public, voluntary and private sectors in which we are well placed to respond with a dynamic solution to see young people experience the love of God. Our vision is to scale to reach a generation of young people and make a transformational difference. We now seek to grow to the fifteen regions of the UK within the next fifteen years.

3. Marvelous God

KICK's Story is written from a Christian worldview. It is not ashamed to marvel at God, who I believe is living and active in this world. I respect other views that are different from my own. However, I would still encourage those who read this book to be open-minded and let the stories wash over you, whether you believe in God or not. Consider how else the outcomes might have happened without a God working things together for good. KICK's stories will describe real-life accounts from our lived experience but will not mention any names or locations of young people, to protect and safeguard them. From this point forward and throughout this book, I will talk about children and young people, but for ease, I will refer to them as "young people." Please note there was much more we could have collected to share. We couldn't mention everyone's contribution to KICK over the years. Still, I trust that those included and those not included understand the spirit with which this book is constructed to showcase the themes of our mission. The book will speak through our experience at KICK; it has looked to engage people from the past and present with a desire to make a difference on behalf of the young people we serve. I would like to state that I am indebted to the many who have helped in the writing of this book and any error of detail or fact that may remain, is entirely my own. I'm a relational person and my natural style is conversational. I hope this reaches you and engages you as a result.

Part of my journey has been a vivid experience of God teaching me stories throughout the whole scripture to which Jesus gives a deeper meaning. I have found reading the Bible cover to cover has been a rich opportunity for God to speak to me during these past years, and so the spiritual applications are drawn from books right through the Bible from the Old and New Testaments. It has been our experience, as in 1 Corinthians 3:6, that Paul planted, Apollos watered, but only God grows spiritual change. Whatever you have been drawn to doing, do it with all you can and then wait on the LORD to bring the increase. I hope this will inspire you to unpack stories of calling and adventures in UK mission that lead you to worship a glorious God.

How to Read this Book

Framed through our organisational values, KICK's Story will present you with paired chapters to see current stories of God's intervention through our work at KICK and then some of the spiritual applications of that value. Starting from a position of mission – the why, how, and what of KICK's work – the following chapters map stories and their spiritual application in pairs through KICK's values to be Aspirational, Compassionate, Excellent, Intentional and Integral (ACEII). We will look at a chapter of stories and then a chapter of spiritual application, expressing what has happened and what God has taught us along the journey. We will address why we value those values and the impact they can make on your life. The stories are our lived experiences at KICK, from trustees to leaders, coaches, mentors, chaplains and volunteers. The spiritual applications are some of what I have learned on this journey. I trust that the stories warm your heart of God's active involvement in the twenty-first century and that you are encouraged by some of the spiritual insights witnessed along this journey. In the excellent biography of James O. Fraser's mission to China, he reflected, "The most unexpected things had been the spiritual secrets, the opening up of the mysteries, I had thought belonged in Heaven. I had little realised how deeply a man could drink of the cup of fellowship with God down here."[4] This has been my experience as we have journeyed, witnessing God's work with us and the spiritual secrets God has revealed. I have treasured these, and I hope and pray this gold also becomes a blessing to you.

PART ONE
| MISSION |

JOE LOWTHER

Chapter 1
Mission: KICK's Story

Mission is the why and the what of an organisation. Mission is essential as the true north of what an organisation desires to do and the change they aspire to bring. Children and young people are struggling, with one-third of sixteen to twenty-four-year-olds in the UK (31%) reporting evidence of depression or anxiety. Therefore, KICK's mission is to transform young people's lives with God's love through sport and support. This drives all our decisions and is the change we seek to bring. Identifying mission as the why of the organisation is a crucial step of faith. Smith Wigglesworth once wrote, "Great faith is a product of great fights. Great testimonies are the outcome of great tests. Great triumphs can only come out of great trials."[5] Therefore, mission as a step of faith is a trial which must be worth fighting and a triumph worth celebrating.

1. Problem, Solution and What Happens If We Fail

Having run a government-funded school, I'd had no previous need to fundraise. However, now I found myself in an organisation with a £60,000 deficit. Wow. KICK would go bust if we didn't secure new income. So, I set about trying to write a fundraising strategy. I came across an article in the Guardian called 'What's Your Problem, Solution and What Happens if You Fail?'[6] It's a helpful guide for fundraising, so I set about mapping KICK's problem. Many young people express a sense of hopelessness, as evidenced by the 1-in-3 that identify with a mental health concern, the ninety-five percent of young people who do not go to church in the UK and the reality that three-out-of-four sixteen to twenty-four-year-olds feel disillusioned with life. Our Solution is our mission to transform young people's lives with God's love through sport and support. If only 4.5% of children and young people go to church, then where are they? Well, 99.1% attend school. So, as a result, we go into schools and deliver values-driven Physical Education, Street Dance Coaching, Solution Focused Mentoring and Schools-based Chaplaincy, and then upskill local people from local churches to reach local young people in their community through KICK Academies, where we train volunteers to coach young people in sport, dance, running or multi-sport and share an inspirational thought from the Bible. We want to replace this sense of hopelessness, with a hope for the future, joy in the present. But then the third question came – what happens if we fail? The hairs on the back of my neck pricked up. Wow, we lose a generation for Jesus. A Scripture sprang to mind in John 9:4 where "Jesus said, 'As long as it is day, we must do the work of Him who sent me. Night is coming when no one can work.'" There is an urgency to our mission. There is a time limit. Two months into the role, I had the privilege of going to the Youth for Christ Conference in Manchester in January 2015, and Wes Stafford, the founder of Compassion International, said that eighty-six percent of people who become Christians give their lives to the Lord before the age of twenty-three. The opportunity for mission is youth. We must act quickly and not miss out on this crucial opportunity to explore faith. God is able, but the time to act is early and the time to act is now.

2. Roots and Fruits

When I first arrived at KICK, there were clearly things we valued, but these needed to be articulated. We ran an exercise with the five coaches in the organisation about how we wanted KICK to operate. We wanted the charity to hold on to what is most crucial: our heart (ethos), our core (values) and what we visibly expect to see from all our staff (behaviours). Our Christian ethos is "To follow the example of Jesus who loved young people and was relevant in the way He communicated with them." This inspires our operational motivations, as we seek to transform young people's lives. If our organisation were a person, we would view our ethos as the heart of the work that we do; the values as the inner body, central, like in Blackpool Rock, where you could look inside one of our coaches and see our values in their core; and then the behaviours as the outward appearance of what people experience as we serve them. We put this in place to demonstrate how the Christian faith underpins the core motivation for the organisation's work and forms the foundation for its culture now and in the future. The basis for our Christian ethos is the Bible, from which the understanding of our KICK Values are inspired and drawn. As we journey through each value in this book, we will look at its importance today and its Biblical basis.

These ACEII Values are to inform how we operate to transform young people's lives by being:

- Aspirational on behalf of our young people, being ambitious for their progress and in our hope to see them succeed,

- Compassionate toward our young people, showing humility, listening to them and making our approach flexible to suit their needs,

- Excellent in our performance, innovating with continuous improvement for the best outcomes for our young people,

- Intentional in our relationships with young people, schools, churches, partners, funders and each other to build a family together at KICK,
- Integral in our decision-making, our interactions with each other and our partnerships.

Our values were conceived by our staff team; they are shared values and behaviours. To celebrate this, we commissioned Stuart Kennett, one of our Senior Coaches, to design a piece of artwork around KICK's ethos and values. He created the image from a silhouette of when Brazilian footballer, Kaka, celebrated winning the European Cup with a T-shirt which read "I belong to Jesus." We wanted KICK's values and ethos to be alive and at the forefront of our work. This image is a visual reminder of their importance.

As we considered our next strategic steps, YWAM's Yan Nichols had a picture when praying for KICK of a strawberry tree. He instructed that a strawberry tree looks different above ground with all shapes and sizes, but it is interconnected at its underground roots. As KICK grows, just like a strawberry tree, things might look different above ground – new regions, with different types of services, delivered by different people – but we needed to keep our roots interconnected. KICK had an opportunity to expand but must remain true to its values like this strawberry tree picture, which has diverse expressions above ground but identical roots beneath the surface. In scaling, staff needed different competencies, shifting from everyone multitasking to creating greater role specialisation and often strong operational, delegation and change management. We have kept this close to our hearts to keep our roots deep within our Christian ethos and our ACEII values.

3. Four KICK Academies

Buoyed by this reality, we set out rebuilding some of what KICK had lost. KICK had a strong foundation in school's work but some of the coaches had lost sight of the missional aspect of the organisation. Early on, I wanted to re-establish the church at the centre. We created a Christian ethos – to follow Jesus' example in the way He loved young people and was relevant in the way He communicated with them. This meant that staff were clear on KICK's DNA. We were a missional organisation.

KICK Academies were going to be a priority once more and I met with each of the seven staff members to outline this strategic intent. So, one Thursday afternoon, I met with Zuko, one of our coaches, for coffee. As we talked, Zuko said, "Oh yeah, my church used to have a KICK Academy; maybe we could reopen it?" Thrilled, I countered, "Maybe we could!" The start of our first new KICK Academy. I was so encouraged. I went to observe Zuko's session that cold and misty November evening. While I breathed icy mist out of my mouth, I watched Zuko's session, and a gentleman came up behind me and looked at me with great suspicion. I wondered, Oh dear, maybe he thinks I'm not welcome. Perhaps he will be "anti" towards our work in his child's school. So, when he barked at me, "What are you doing here?" I felt like my fears were revealed. I shared about KICK's general work in schools and then gulped and went further to discuss our work with churches. As I did, his eyebrows raised, and I worried he was getting more and more suspicious and upset. All the way through to a climax of a response... "Well, this is great, as I am an operations manager for a local church. I'd love to have a new KICK Academy at our church. How soon can we train volunteers?" Wow. Two KICK Academies in two hours! As we left the school, I felt elated that God was doing something and rebirthing KICK Academies. Then I got a phone call from our Operations Manager at KICK – Jo Bradbury. "A gentleman called Steve Bryers has called to explore setting up a KICK Academy." Steve Bryers – the same Steve Bryers who I'd recruited to my old school and who had moved to Brazil on mission two years previously – had come back to the UK and unbeknown to both of us, had found out about KICK and contacted us to explore working together. Three KICK Academies, three hours?! When I arrived home and turned the gate, I got a phone call from a friend. "Hi Joe, it's Laura. My husband has just become a youth worker in Putney and would love to set up a KICK Academy at our church. Four KICK Academies in four hours! God is good and He was speaking.

4. Faith is Spelt "Risk"

KICK Academies were on the move as God breathed new life into KICK. Schools work was next, and we started to see the LORD expand our reach. Hans Sims had previously worked for KICK from 2006–2009. We had grown up together and interestingly I brought Hans across to City Gateway to lead on sports provision. Now, at KICK myself, I realised KICK had a Hans-shaped hole. We needed developed infrastructure to grow. Hans was the ideal leader to build strong foundations. However, we had a £60,000 budget deficit. Employing Hans would increase this by fifty percent. Hans said he was keen to join/re-join, but I felt the pressure of bringing him across in case we went under straight away. So, we committed to pray. I wanted clarity from the Lord. The night of the decision, I asked for prayer at my church, Christian Fellowship in Richmond. I explained the situation and said I didn't know what to do. Church Elder, Gbenga Anojobi, said boldly, "God will tell you before you make the decision." In that moment of faith, I knew a peace that God would. God gave me Philippians 4:1–7 which says,

"Therefore, my brothers and sisters, you whom I love and long for, my joy and crown, stand firm in the Lord in this way, dear friends! I plead with Euodia and I plead with Syntyche to be of the same mind in the Lord. Yes, and I ask you, my true companion, help these women since they have contended at my side in the cause of the Gospel, along with Clement and the rest of my co-workers, whose names are in the book of life. Rejoice in the Lord always. I will say it again: Rejoice! Let your gentleness be evident to all. The Lord is near. Do not be anxious about anything, but in every situation, by prayer and petition, with thanksgiving, present your requests to God. And the peace of God, which transcends all understanding, will guard your hearts and your minds in Christ Jesus."

Hans was like family, a true brother and a dear friend with whom I could stand firm (v1). We needed to be of the same mind in this step of faith (v2); it would help Jo Bradbury, a woman who contended for the faith (v3), and it was for the sake of the Gospel (v4). A deep sense of peace descended over me that God would provide. Our Chair, Matt King, agreed, as did Hans when we spoke. We stepped out in faith and miraculously ended the year with a breakeven budget. God was so good, and in those early years of my time at KICK, Hans was instrumental in growing the organisation's quality, Christian ethos, and missional heartbeat. Faith can be spelt as "risk".

5. Sport's Cultural Capital

We can see the powerful impact that sport can bring. A third of all professional football teams were founded by local churches, often in slums, as an approach to restore the social and spiritual good of those communities. Sport gathers people to participate, and it inspires the imagination. It is a powerful opportunity to connect with culture and all that it means to be human. Sport brings to the fore the physical, mental and emotional.

At KICK, we can see the opportunity to share sporting stories to develop young people. A great example of forgiveness is found in boxing with Michael Watson. In 1991, Watson collapsed at the end of his World

Championship fight with Chris Eubank. He was in a coma for forty days, and a blood clot in his brain left him partially paralysed. Watson later said: "I prayed for strength, and I prayed for Chris Eubank. I knew he was suffering. I didn't feel angry toward him because it could have happened either way."

In 1969, golf's Ryder Cup reached its climax when Britain's Tony Jacklin and American Jack Nicklaus arrived at the eighteenth hole all-square with the overall scores tied. Jacklin faced a three-footer to earn the first-ever tie in the event. In a show of integrity, instead of forcing his rival to take his shot, Nicklaus picked up Jacklin's ball marker and conceded the tie. "I don't think you would have missed that Tony," Nicklaus said, "but I didn't want to give you the chance." This example demonstrates gentleness and the importance of not winning at all costs.

A further case we use with young people is from synchronised swimming, where at the World Championships in Budapest in 2023, USA's Anita Alvarez sank to the bottom of the pool. Her coach, Andrea Fuentes, realising something was wrong, immediately dove in after her, pulling Alvarez to safety. If Andrea had not noticed, she would have drowned. We use this story to communicate the importance of kindness and watching out for your teammates.

Another illustration from the 2016 Triathlon World Series in Mexico is that, with seven hundred metres left of his triathlon, Great Britain's Jonny Brownlee collapsed with exhaustion. His brother Alistair was in second place but stopped to help his brother over the finish line in a dramatic end to the race. This profound show of brotherly love cost Alistair a gold medal but it can speak to young people about the opportunity to show compassion. We can see the missional opportunity to go through sport to reach young people.

6. Adding Mentoring and Chaplaincy

We began to see the need grow around young people's mental health. We piloted mentoring provision and were inspired to use the Solutions Focused approach to mentoring by the brilliant Dani Knox. Solutions Focused Mentoring builds on Cognitive Behavioural Therapy (CBT) principles to help young people find the solutions to the problems they face. We heard time and time again moving stories of lives impacted by the words of a mentor. However, we determined not to overstep any line or impose faith. So, mentoring was just for personal and social issues, not faith discussions. This led us to explore Chaplaincy. Tom Rutter had felt he needed a new challenge after fifteen years at KICK. Then, that Friday, I got a call from the school, where Tom worked, to say they would like a new Chaplain and asked if we could ever provide Chaplaincy. Hilarious?! We could say yes right away, and Tom became the school chaplain.

In his first week as school chaplain, tragically, a lady with a mental health problem set herself on fire, ran out of her estate and died in front of the school gates. From that moment, Tom knew how vital his new role was – to pastor parents, teachers and pupils who had witnessed this horrific incident. Starting this provision in 2019, ahead of what was to come with the lockdown era, was God's timing as Tom played a courageous role in provision working with young people who experienced so much pain. Not to mention attending the gates of committal for a learner who took her life but, due to social distancing, could only have ten people at the funeral. Tom met with learners who wanted to attend but couldn't and kept a distance for the family to grieve. He remembers, "This was a terrible shock for students and staff. The isolation and disconnection that both young people and adults experienced during the Lockdowns created environments where young people who were suffering saw taking their own lives as the only option. These individuals need the support and connection that helps show them that there are other pathways ahead. To cater to people's needs, we must respond with specific mental, physical, emotional and spiritual support."

7. A Sustainable Model

So, during this period, we grew our work from 2014 to 2019 from seven staff to thirty staff, growing from two thousand five hundred young people per week to ten thousand and twelve. We delivered PE, dance, mentoring and chaplaincy, for which schools paid to provide our professional services. Building upon that, we trained local church volunteers to run additional KICK Academies. Our testimony was that "God's work, when done in God's way, never lacked God's resources."[7] Stepping forward in faith, we felt drawn to go national and grow outside of London. I took a Masters in Change Management for charities in preparation, graduating in January 2020, just ahead of an era which would test our faith to the maximum… Lockdown.

Summary

These stories of God's engagement in our work grew our faith in His ability to deliver our mission to transform young people's lives. We can't and don't want to deliver our mission without His engagement, involvement and love. As we saw God's fingerprints on our work, we saw the spiritual reality that God is a Master Builder.

JOE LOWTHER

Chapter 2
Mission: Spiritual Application

What spiritual lessons did we learn during this period of KICK's evolution? It was the reality that in mission, God is a Master Builder. I use this turn of phase in relation to the spiritual reality that God is specifically at work amongst each generation. He is accurate, purposeful and precise in every detail of His design and planning. Not that He is inflexible in His building, but that He cares, is intentional and purposeful in the plans He makes and directs. As Psalm 33:11 declares, "The plans of the Lord stand firm forever, the purposes of His heart through all generations." God is a grand architect whose purposes work through fallible people despite us, and whose plans stand firm forever. This chapter will map the reality of how God demonstrated this to us in KICK's story. I trust and pray that the lessons we learnt about mission will apply to your life as you read this and apply the principles yourself.

1. God is Not Far Away

God is a Master Builder. He is the creator of the heavens and the earth. But He is also the God who knit us together in our mother's womb. God is into remarkable design, and we can see this with the miracle of tiny fingernails on the minuscule fingers of new born babies. However, when we think about God, do we imagine a God far away? Do we think of a God who is far off and asleep? Do we dare to consider that God is engaged in this world and actively looking to build His Kingdom?

Psalm 11:4-5 says, "The Lord is in His holy temple; the Lord is on His heavenly throne. He observes everyone on earth; His eyes examine them." Here, the Lord is not asleep; He is watching everyone intently. He examines people's hearts – He is focused and committed in His intent, and those who are right before Him will see Him face to face. What a privilege: God is not distant; He is involved and wants a relationship with you. God cares about how you act, what you think, what is in your heart. As we see in Ephesians 5:14–16, "This is why it is said: 'Wake up, sleeper, rise from the dead, and Christ will shine on you.' Be very careful, then, how you live – not as unwise but as wise, making the most of every opportunity, because the days are evil." Instead of God being asleep, the truth is that we are often blind to the spiritual reality of what is going on in this world. Jesus wants to shine His light on us to help us engage and be missionally purposeful in our lives. God is close, not far off and wants us to take every opportunity to be missionally effective.

2. God is a Master Builder

The Bible is overflowing with real-life case studies from which we can learn from God's engagement with people and desire to know us. As our heavenly father, who was prepared to send His own son to salvage us all for a restored relationship with Him, God wants to build His Kingdom with us and build it accurately. Consider these examples: Noah building the Ark (Genesis 6–9); Conquering the Fortress of Jericho (Joshua 2–6); Gideon defeating the Midianites (Judges 6–8); Nathan prophesying for King David (1 Chronicles 17:1–15); and the specificity of design for building the Temple (2 Chronicles 3).

Let's read 2 Chronicles 6:7–9, "My father David had it in his heart to build a temple for the name of the Lord, the God of Israel. But the Lord said to my father David, 'You did well to have it in your heart to build a temple for My name. Nevertheless, you are not the one to build the temple, but your son, your own flesh and blood – he is the one who will build the temple for My name.'"

God has plans and as a Master Builder, He especially cares not only about the specific material for building His Temple but the specific people He wants in His work. An example of this was when I joined KICK and one of our coaches questioned if we could fully deliver Physical Education as technically, we needed to offer dance. Now we had excellent sports coaches but some of them were dreadful dancers. Sport and dance are very distinctive areas and need their own specialist coaches. So, we set about conjuring up dance from scratch. At a leadership course at Bayes Business School, I worked with other students to design dance as an innovation for KICK. We developed the concept through total strangers, with fantastic insights from Youth for Christ's Grace Wheeler. I then started pitching Street Dance to headteachers without a dance coach or curriculum in sight. Again, stepping forward in faith, we identified someone who offered them the role, and then they turned it down to go on tour. Then, another new person accepted the post and pulled out two weeks before summer. I got on the phone and called all kinds of different leads, desperate for someone to fulfil the contracts we have signed for schools. We got three interviews, but only one turned up, and she was brilliant. We offered the job, and the next day, she said her current employer had begged her to stay and that she'd not be coming. Three days before the summer holidays. Disaster.

This was the single most stressful recruitment drive I had ever encountered. How could we find a specialist street dance coach in no time? We prayed, and I put on Facebook a message: "Desperate: KICK is recruiting a new street dance coach. Please help me find someone who loves Jesus and loves dance." It was a tough evening; I felt helpless to do anything. As I scrolled through social media that evening, I came across a T-shirt which read, "Being a CEO is as easy as riding a bike, but the bike is on fire and going off a cliff." My feeling about it exactly.

Miraculously, though, God had a game plan, and we incredibly had three more applicants by His grace. Two could make the Friday, but the third could only make the Saturday. Both Friday applicants dropped out to leave on the last chance – Rachel Hollings. I interviewed Rachel at 11am on the Saturday I was meant to be driving to Dorset. The interview was only meant to be thirty minutes but lasted two hours. It was a brilliant meeting of minds. Rachel is a genuinely gifted dance coach with a love for life and a passion for young people. Agreed to join KICK, and we'd done, no God had done it, in the nick of time. Rachel has since gone on to work for KICK for eight years and is still with KICK today. We praise God for Rachel and see how she was the best possible person to have joined KICK. Rachel was worth the wait, and it is worth waiting for God's specific pieces to complete His jigsaw.

3. We Have Choices

God also knows the hearts of people as He builds. Our hearts can resist His plans. Psalm 10 demonstrates the specificity of how God can read the hearts of humankind.

Psalm 10:2–4,11, 14, 17–18 says, "In his arrogance the wicked man hunts down the weak, who are caught in the schemes he devises. He boasts about the cravings of his heart; he blesses the greedy and reviles the Lord. In his pride the wicked man does not seek him; in all his thoughts there is no room for God. He says to himself, 'God will never notice; he covers his face and never sees.' But You, God, see the trouble of the afflicted; You consider their grief and take it in hand. The victims commit themselves to You; You are the helper of the fatherless. You, Lord, hear the desire of the afflicted; You encourage them, and you listen to their cry, defending the fatherless and the oppressed, so that mere earthly mortals will never again strike terror."

Mission is not ours. Mission is God's. It is "Thy Kingdom come", not "my kingdom come" or anyone else's. He builds One Kingdom, not many. We can choose to be a part of that or go with our own schemes. In following God's work and in God's ways, we can rely on Him to provide the resources. Anything else means we are on our own. In Mark 1:40–45, Jesus could not do miracles in a town because a man He healed of leprosy gossiped freely about it, which meant the mission was held up. In mission, we need to do exactly what God tells us to do rather than what we think is best. We felt challenged by the caution of Ecclesiastes 7:29, "This only have I found: God created mankind upright, but they have gone in search of many schemes." At KICK, we have learnt that everything God specifically asks us to do is more meaningful than when we simply go to do something and then simply ask God to bless it after we have made the decision and actioned it! As Abraham Lincoln helpfully reflected, "Sir, my concern is not whether God is on my side; my greatest concern is to be on God's side, for God is always right."[8] God has specific plans; we can ask Him for guidance of what they are and He will show us the right steps as we follow Him.

4. God Wants to Build Masterfully With You!

God's approach is masterful and fascinatingly so; He wants to do this with and through you. We see this with the old nation of Israel as an example to us in the specificity of how God wanted King Solomon to project manage in detail the building of the temple.

2 Chronicles 7:11–22

"When Solomon had finished the temple of the Lord and the royal palace and had succeeded in carrying out all he had in mind to do in the temple of the Lord and in his own palace, the Lord appeared to him at night and said, 'I have heard your prayer and have chosen this place for Myself as a temple for sacrifices. When I shut up the heavens so that there is no rain, or command locusts to devour the land or send a plague among My people, if My people, who are called by My name, will humble themselves and pray and seek My face and turn from their wicked ways, then I will hear from heaven, and I will forgive their sin and will heal their land. Now My eyes will be open and My ears attentive to the prayers offered in this place. I have chosen and consecrated this temple so that My name may be there forever. My eyes and My heart will always be there. As for you, if you walk before Me faithfully as David your father did, and do all I command, and observe My decrees and laws, I will establish your royal throne, as I covenanted with David your father when I said, 'You shall never fail to have a successor to rule over Israel.' But if you turn away and forsake the decrees and commands I have given you and go off to serve other gods and worship them, then I will uproot Israel from My land, which I have given them and will reject this temple I have consecrated for My name. I will make it a byword and an object of ridicule among all peoples. This temple will become a heap of rubble. All who pass by will be appalled and say, 'Why has the Lord done such a thing to this land and to this temple?' People will answer, 'Because they have forsaken the Lord, the God of their ancestors, who brought them out of Egypt, and have embraced other gods, worshiping and serving them – that is why He brought all this disaster on them.'"

As with the case study, God speaks into and across time. Will we listen to Him in our own lives? We can be a part of His grand design together with Him. Are you clear that you are today inside the overview of the Bible? Creation has happened; God worked through the Israelite people, and then Jesus came to redeem a lost people. Paul brought the Gospel to us Gentiles, but Jesus has not yet returned as prophesied and demonstrated in Revelation. We have got this to come. We are inside His great big picture. As with my story of arriving at KICK, where He called me to leave my job ahead of providing a new one. This terrified me, but God had it covered and, rather than leave me hanging, honoured me and those around me with a strong Ofsted result. He wants us to listen and work with Him. God will use you as He changes you. You don't have to be perfect at the start but Jesus as the Good Shepherd, will guide you in His ways. He has prepared good works for us in advance to do. Will we seek Him to find out what these are? Do we realise that He wants to equip us for the task?

We see that anything is possible with God, as He determines. We are to find His will and can draw insight from Psalm 18:29–36, "With Your help I can advance against a troop; with my God I can scale a wall. As for God, His way is perfect: The Lord's word is flawless; He shields all who take refuge in Him. For who is God besides the Lord? And who is the Rock except our God? It is God who arms me with strength and keeps my way secure. He makes my feet like the feet of a deer; He causes me to stand on the heights. He trains my hands for battle; my arms can bend a bow of bronze. You make Your saving help my shield, and Your right hand sustains me; Your help has made me great. You provide a broad path for my feet, so that my ankles do not give way."

Summary

God has specific plans. His mission is flawless. No one has the strategic mind of God, nor the strength to wholly shield or the ability to keep their way entirely secure. Trust the Master Builder. We have a choice to follow or go our own way. Ecclesiastes 8:13 sets these risks of not listening and following God, "Yet because the wicked do not fear God, it will not go well with them, and their days will not lengthen like a shadow." Jude 19 further articulates, "These are the people who divide you, who follow mere natural instincts and do not have the Spirit." Will we follow our natural instincts, schemes or worldly paths in mission? Or are we prepared to listen to the Master Builder, be inspired by Jesus' intercession and walk by the Spirit in reverence to God to see the masterpiece of His thrilling plans? Whatever the mission is, let's count it as a privilege to listen, understand and follow the works God has prepared in advance for us to do. We may remain anxious and even scared at times about following Him in the manner and direction He requires, but if we ask God, He gives the courage to overcome such fears to do His will.

JOE LOWTHER

PART TWO
| ASPIRATION |

JOE LOWTHER

Chapter 3
Aspiration: KICK's Story

Aspiration is the first of what KICK values most. We want to be aspirational on behalf of the young people we serve. Many young people are abandoning their dreams and ambitions. They feel hopeless due to the cost-of-living crisis and mental health concerns, with half of those in one survey stating they were not able to think beyond the next six months.[9] We need to hold hope for those who have no hope, so that they grow into holding aspirations for themselves. Jesus believed in young people and respected children and what they had to offer. He said, "I praise You, Father, Lord of heaven and earth, because You have hidden these things from the wise and learned and revealed them to little children" (Matthew 11:25). Jesus was not too proud to spend time with children or too pompous, instead rebuking those close to Him whom He challenged to draw close and listen to young people. Jesus even said that it is to children that the Kingdom of Heaven belongs (Matthew 19:13–14). God values young people – they are not insignificant – saying, "From the lips of children and infants You, Lord, have called forth Your praise" (Matthew 21:16). Jesus went further in His manifesto of how much He loves children calling adults to become like children when in relation to being proud and in their place before God (John 12:36). Jesus refers to all Christians as "children of God" and now we can of course still be children of our parents well into our later years as adults – so this is not exclusively to child-aged listeners but the principle is our need for dependency on our heavenly

Father. But it is also instructive that God wants us to relate well to young people and engage them. Therefore, we want to be aspirational on behalf of young people as Jesus was. We desire to grow to make a transformational difference in their lives. We were so encouraged by what God had done at KICK that our trustees were inspired by a new vision to take the organisation national.

1. Dreaming a Dream

Matt King, KICK Chair of Trustees, shares how he felt drawn to a new vision to reach a generation within a generation of time.

"In November 2018, I was on a flight to Singapore for work; I read a book with the following challenge: 'What are you dreaming for? Because when the world says you can't, God says you can.' His message was inspired by Ephesians 3:20–21, 'Now to Him who is able to do immeasurably more than all we ask or imagine, according to His power that is at work within us, to Him be glory in the church and in Christ Jesus throughout all generations, forever and ever! Amen.'

"'Matt', the book shouted out, 'What is your dream? What dream can God do immeasurably more than you can ever imagine?' I boarded the second leg from Singapore to Melbourne. I decided to write a prayer for an audacious dream that only God could deliver. To pray that He would do immeasurably more than I could ever imagine or dream. That night when I was very much awake, I had a dream.

"Twelve years earlier, I was driving my car along a busy road, and I had a thought to build an organisation that employed five thousand coaches, who in turn would each interact with about one thousand two hundred young people each week in schools, through coaching, mentoring and support, which in turn would connect with about six million young people. To give every child the opportunity to make an informed decision about Jesus' love for them. So, I devoted my charitable time to developing KICK to deliver this dream, providing a vision. We have had fantastic success engaging with, at the time, over ten thousand young people every week. However, it was nowhere near the six million young people I had dreamt about in 2006.

"To be honest, I had totally forgotten about these thoughts. When you chair a charity, the day-to-day work becomes all about monthly accounts, chairing board meetings, and dealing with problems and these challenges can be full-on and more than I can sometimes cope with. And so the thoughts from twelve years ago had evaporated. But there I was in Australia in 2018, having gotten off a flight and read Brian Houston's book, asking me, 'Matt, what is your dream?'

"As I lay in bed with jetlag, unable to sleep, my daughter Hannah called me at about 02:00 and said, 'Dad, please could you help me with my third year university Theology essay on the secularisation of the UK through the impact of the First World War on six million soldiers?"

"My heart sunk... I had no idea what to say! But at that moment in a Melbourne hotel room... five hours after getting off the plane, having asked God for a dream.... I felt my dream from twelve years earlier rise within me.

The secularisation of six million soldiers... I had dreamt twelve years earlier about giving six million young people an opportunity to explore God's love for them through Jesus. My dream had been reignited. Matt... what is your dream? My dream is to give every young person the opportunity to make an informed decision and choice about God's love through Jesus. "I called the CEO, Joe Lowther, the following morning to tell him about my dream. The next day, Joe attended a conference at Lambeth Palace, where the head of the sports ministry for the Church of England was presenting his vision for sport within the UK. At the end of his presentation, he approached Joe and the CEO of Christians in Sport and said, 'I believe that a Christian sports coach should be placed in every parish in the UK.' When Joe told me that the following day, I was immensely relieved.

"I had spent the day racking my consulting brain on how to deliver the dream God had given me. When Joe told me that the head of the sports ministry for the Church of England had suggested that someone else see a similar vision, it highlighted to me that God could do more than I can hope or imagine and certainly more than I can deliver myself.

"If God is in it, the vision can be delivered in a way that is different from how I might try to do it. Since then, I have been encouraged that God can do it without me worrying too much. Our CEO has translated this into a plan to engage a generation within a generation, and we are making significant progress towards this dream."

2. Lockdown Salvation

As we have seen, God is a Master Builder. God had given us the vision but we needed to look to Him to reveal the next steps of the plans. We felt (and still do) both inspired and terrified by the enormity of this aspirational challenge: To reach a generation of young people within a generation of time. To go to the fifteen regions of the UK in the next fifteen years transformed a nation.

As CEO, I considered it and thought we needed one more year to get everything in place, but the task's urgency challenged me. So, in 2019, we started to prepare to go national in 2020; but COVID-19 arrived across the world early that year. In mid-March, the Prime Minister announced that all the schools were closing. We anticipated it would be for a month, including Easter. The PM said, "for the foreseeable future." We thought, "Oh no." We have 3.5 months reserves but not six months. Maybe this is the end? The lockdown was announced on a Wednesday night and sank in for us on Thursday. Matt King brilliantly urged me to go for broke and speak with all seventy headteachers on the Friday. I have never been more nervous. But I kept running Psalm 121:1–2 through my head and my heart, "I lift my eyes up to the mountains, where does my help come from? My help comes from the Lord, the Maker of heaven and earth." We rang seventy headteachers as a last hope. We levelled with the headteachers to "Please stand by us, or we might not be here after the lockdown." We were blown away by the feedback from headteachers saying how much they loved KICK and wanted to stand by us.

As the Lord would have it, that Friday morning at midnight, the Government had informed schools they had to set up Key Worker provision. Instead of dropping KICK, these headteachers were delighted we'd rung so that we could run their Key Worker education for them. During this crisis, we miraculously continued to work in fifty-eight of our seventy-one schools. Whilst all the schools were supposed to have been shut, we delivered sport, dance and chaplaincy on-site to government-designated Key Worker children to enable their parents to go out and save lives. We also pivoted to deliver Remote Mentoring, offering sessions online to engage those most at risk dealing with issues such as anxiety, maintaining positive thinking, contributing an active part in home life, keeping a good routine and structure and providing purpose and stimulation throughout the day. We lifted our eyes up to the mountains and our help came from the Lord. He was not asleep or slumbering, but was there for us, watching over us, keeping us from bankruptcy and tasking us to serve strategically for children and their families during the pandemic. What a Master Builder!

3. God Wants You to Walk With Him

Lockdown felt like a rollercoaster. There had been so many ups and downs. Some schools dropped us; we had to put some staff on Furlough, one of our coach's younger brothers died of COVID-19 aged just twenty-five and hearing of the impossible pressures of our young people. It was a hard time, but God graciously gave us Isaiah 33 as comfort.

"Lord, be gracious to us; we long for you. Be our strength every morning, our salvation in time of distress. The Lord is exalted, for He dwells on high, He will fill Zion with His justice and righteousness. He will be the sure foundation for Your times, a rich store of salvation and wisdom and knowledge; the fear of the Lord is the key to this treasure."

The Lord can strengthen us every morning to do things we can't cope with. He is a sure foundation for us to stand on in uncertain times. We can engage the rich store of salvation, wisdom and knowledge when we fear the Lord. The key to this treasure is to revere the Lord. It means walking in step with Him, honouring Him, talking with Him. He wants to give us not cheap but rich stores of salvation in our circumstances, wisdom to navigate them and knowledge as to how to act in hard times. We don't know why COVID-19 happened but we do know that God was not asleep. He was wide awake and on the throne. He is an ever-present help in times of trouble. He wants to give you salvation, wisdom and knowledge in struggles. Things may get harder before they get better, but we learnt that He wants us to trust Him through faith. God wants you to walk with Him. Walk in step with the Holy Spirit. Life is a marathon; walk, don't sprint. Look to God for your aspiration by lifting your eyes up and knowing where your help comes from (Psalm 121), remembering He's wide awake and has a rich store of salvation, wisdom and knowledge ready to strengthen you each morning (Isaiah 33).

4. Light Fires Across the UK

Inspired by God's provision to save KICK from an existential crisis, we saw that KICK had been preserved for a purpose, and we needed to respond. Secondly, the national need had dramatically increased for young people with a new mental health pandemic, following the eight hundred and forty million days of education that had been lost during the lockdowns.[10] Thirdly, Zoom literacy has brought the nation closer together geographically. Suddenly, I could be in the North East, West Midlands, East of England and London within a morning via Zoom. Zoom brought a massive shift in speeding a national expansion that didn't previously exist. Now, things were ready. Also, I was grateful to have had the extra year of bedding in new managers to prepare to go national. God's timing is perfect. We built on the vision God had given Matt King and looked at the opportunity to light fires across the UK, exploring moving to five new regions in five years. We would realise our aspiration to expand out of London to go to the West Midlands, East Midlands and East of England in year one and then onto the North West and North East of England.

5. God's Timing and Northwest

As we pressed on with going national, this coincided with news that the Church of England would appoint a National Sports Ministry lead and have seven pilot Diocese. The wonderful Natalie Andrews was a colossal help in introducing KICK to Bishops, Education Directors and Mission Leads in the new regions we expanded into. As we grew, we worked with churches from a wide range of denominations, such as Baptists, Methodists, Elim, Assemblies of God, New Frontiers, Redeemed Christian Church of God and many others. When we went to the North West, I spoke at the Blackburn Headteachers Conference, where there was massive interest in KICK's work. On my way home, I thought, how exciting, but equally, how would we recruit new coaches in this new region? I got a phone call from our HR Manager, Becci Lee, sharing some sad news: one of our coaches was planning on moving to Blackburn part-time, but would KICK ever consider going there so they could continue working for KICK? Although the plans turned out differently in the end, this gave us encouragement that God was with us and weaving things together behind the scenes.

In another situation, other new coaches for North West pulled out just before we started provision. We cried out in prayer for God to provide. Risking our reputation in the new area, we urgently contacted the community. I was introduced to a church leader at Beacon Church. They shared that they had a great youth worker, but they could no longer afford to pay full time to work for them. Could KICK ever employ them part-time and they retain him part-time? "Of course," I said, "When can I meet him?" The church leader said, "Well, he's on paternity leave, and we have been praying that we would meet to start the redundancy process on his first day back. I waited desperately for him to join and was bowled over when we met, and he said, "I had a prophesy when I was younger that God would use me in sports ministry, and I'd been wondering how God would do it." We employed him and three other people within a nine-day turnaround. God's timing was again perfect.

6. God Was the Driver

The final piece of the jigsaw was a need for the funding to go national. We needed start-up costs of £251,000. Fundraising a quarter of a million pounds was daunting but we knew a peace that God would provide. If it was His mission and if He was the Master Builder, He would provide what was needed. So, we met at the March Board meeting in 2021 to confirm that we would go national to the five new regions of the UK. Within a week, forty percent of the fundraising target came in with a £75,000 application, and a £26,000 application came in with a blessing to go national. Then, three months later, in July, we were given £150,000 by the Benefact Trust. All the money had come in before the new academic year, when we went national. God was so good.

KICK's work proliferated from engaging ten thousand and twelve to twenty-eight thousand six hundred and sixty-eight young people per week in three years across a hundred and thirteen schools and twenty-five KICK Academies. We had innovated new services in schools to develop our provision from six sport disciplines to offer forty different sport and dance disciplines. Our mentoring provision has grown from twenty-two young people in 2015 to one thousand two hundred and sixty-one per week in 2024. In July 2023, we saw one hundred and one young people chose to become Christians. We were all clear that this vision that God had given was miraculously taking place and that God was bringing the increase.

Summary

The aeroplane dream, the Lockdown salvation and lighting fires across the UK all pointed towards a new aspirational vision to reach a generation of young people within a generation of time. We stepped into this vision fuelled by the wind of His aspiration. We felt called to make an aspirational difference to bring young people a hope for the future.

JOE LOWTHER

Chapter 4
Aspiration: Spiritual Application

Aspiration to serve others is an integral part of the spiritual walk. We need to be alert and ready to respond when God calls us. What was the last thing that God said to you as you read the Bible, prayed or through friends in church? How did you respond? What did you do? Did you do anything about it? We will look at three examples from the book of Exodus about Moses, Pharoah and the Israelite people. What was their reaction when God spoke, revealed Himself or intervened in their lives? What were their reactions, and as we reflect on this, what would your response be if this happened to you? What should their or our response be when God speaks, reveals or rescues? As we explore this, consider how you will respond in the faith of aspiration when God next calls you.

1. Moses Looks Towards God

We have an incredible account of God speaking to Moses through a burning bush in Exodus 3:1–22. The context is that God protected Moses as he was born when Egypt was ethnically cleansing Israelite baby boys, then elevated him to a senior position in Pharoah's palace in Egypt as an adult. However, the Israelite people remained in the harsh environment of slavery. Moses saw what was wrong and decided to take the law into his own hands with slave drivers and killed one of them. While we may not have committed a crime, have you ever been frustrated with an injustice and wanted to resolve it but jumped in without taking it to the Lord? God wants us to trust Him and partner together. He sometimes answers us right away, other times He says no, or other times asks us to wait. Moses acted out of his anger, and the consequence was a life had been taken and now Moses had to go on the run to protect his.

Moses spent the following years of his life in the wilderness. He lost his confidence. He went from an adopted heir to the throne to a sheep herder in the desert. Moses threw his life away, but God was not done with him – even as a murderer. It may not have been God's will or Plan A, but despite us, "God works all things together for the good of those who love Him" (Romans 8). People fail, but God's love and purposes for us are never thwarted. God had forgiven Moses and had aspirational plans for His people.

"Now Moses was tending the flock of Jethro, his father-in-law, the priest of Midian, and he led the flock to the far side of the wilderness and came to Horeb, the mountain of God. There, the angel of the Lord appeared to him in flames of fire from within a bush. Moses saw that though the bush was on fire, it did not burn up. So Moses thought, 'I will go over and see this strange sight – why the bush does not burn up.' When the Lord saw that he had gone over to look, God called to him from within the bush, 'Moses! Moses!' And Moses said, 'Here I am.' 'Do not come any closer,' God said. 'Take off your sandals, for the place where you are standing is holy ground.' Then He said, 'I am the God of your father, the God of Abraham, the God of Isaac and the God of Jacob.' At this, Moses hid his face because he was afraid to look at God." – Exodus 3:1–6

In Exodus 3, we see that the Angel of the Lord sets fire to the bush in verse two; God watches to see if Moses responds. Does he turn away and walk off, or does Moses look to see what God might be doing? In verse three, Moses takes a closer look, and in verse four, God speaks to Moses. Sometimes, God wants us to take small steps of faith before He asks us to take bigger ones. God says, "Moses, Moses": Moses' subsequent response is, "Here I am." This is the exact response God wants: our attention, and then to walk towards Him. Then He wants us to recognise Him and be available to Him. Once God has Moses' attention, He reveals a more profound truth in verse five: not to come any closer because He is on holy ground. God then introduces Himself to Moses. This account is so familiar that we might all know that God may speak through bushes. However, imagine how weird this was for Moses, who had no idea until God revealed it was Him. What was Moses' response? Was it as an entitled Egyptian heir? No. In verse six he hid his face in fear and reverence of God. Moses had been humbled and in faith, he responded with awe before God. If today you feel unworthy or unsure how God will call you – humble yourself and listen out for Him.

2. Moses Listens to God's Call

Then in Exodus 3:7–15 we read, "The Lord said, 'I have indeed seen the misery of my people in Egypt. I have heard them crying out because of their slave drivers, and I am concerned about their suffering. So I have come down to rescue them from the hand of the Egyptians and to bring them up out of that land into a good and spacious land, a land flowing with milk and honey – the home of the Canaanites, Hittites, Amorites, Perizzites, Hivites and Jebusites. And now the cry of the Israelites has reached me, and I have seen the way the Egyptians are oppressing them. So now, go. I am sending you to Pharaoh to bring my people the Israelites out of Egypt.' But Moses said to God, 'Who am I that I should go to Pharaoh and bring the Israelites out of Egypt?' And God said, 'I will be with you. And this will be the sign to you that it is I who have sent you: When you have brought the people out of Egypt, you will worship God on this mountain.' Moses said to God, 'Suppose I go to the Israelites and say to them, 'The God of your fathers has sent me to you,' and they ask me, 'What is His name?' Then what shall I tell them?' God said to Moses, 'I am who I am. This is what you are to say to the Israelites: 'I am has sent me to you.'' God also said to Moses, 'Say to the Israelites, 'The Lord, the God of your fathers – the God of Abraham, the God of Isaac and the God of Jacob – has sent me to you.' This is my name forever, the name you shall call Me from generation to generation.'"

As Moses reacted in the right ways to God in taking a closer look, offering himself and being in awe of the Lord, God identified with the pain that Moses had been feeling in the years before for the Israelite people and shared His plan to save them verse seven to ten. Moses reacts to God, questioning God's logic in using him to save the Israelites (v11). Have you ever had questions about how your life might end up? Especially if God has asked you to do something you can't do without His help? God's answer in verse 12 is magnificent: "I will be with you." God will demonstrate His power by working through Moses to bring the Israelites out of slavery. Again, don't forget who Moses was at this point. He was a once most privileged but now unconvicted murderer, who herded sheep in the desert on the run from the law. God was offering to bring him back to Egypt, to save the Israelites from the most powerful empire on the planet! Egypt was the superpower of the day. A colossal call with massive implications both for Moses and also his people. In verse thirteen Moses is faithful in his response, asking how to approach the questions others will have. When you believe the Spirit of God is asking you to do something, be prepared, think it through, pray and ask Him for insight into the areas you don't fully understand. Don't worry if you get it wrong at first, try again and ask Him to show you how. Be humble in trying to seek out God's purposes, learn to listen, choose His direction, prayerfully and then in, in faith, commit to the next steps.

In verse eleven, Moses says, "Who am I..." to take on God's gigantic task! However, in verse fourteen, God's answer to Moses is to tell him and the people who He is. "I AM WHO I AM. I AM has sent you." God earth-shatteringly and illuminatingly reveals that this task is too much for a man to do but requires God. God is with Moses, and He will make it happen. Who is Moses? But God is the I AM. From verse sixteen to twenty-two, God outlines His strategy with Moses, explaining how Moses can be confident because God will give him favour with the Israelite elders, work in power to break Pharaoh's resistance and lead the people out of Egypt.

God had tested Moses to see where his heart was at: was it hardened or open to Him? Moses was called and didn't harden his heart to the Lord. There can be critical moments in our lives. Key turning points. What is our Godly aspiration for His work in our lives? What do we say to the Lord when He calls us? How do we respond when He speaks to us? I have read a helpful book called 'Pursuing God's Will Together'[11] about how to discern the will of God. The book describes a sense of spiritual desolation or consolation when making important decisions. Using these terms I have found that desolation can be experienced when you have to make a difficult decision that is costly to you and makes you feel like death inside, deep in your gut. The sense of consolation is when you pray and make a tough decision in faith, and although it is hard, you feel a deep sense of life and peace. It is here that Moses knew that obeying God would be tough but was assured that God would be with him. This took time, and he struggled, but the more he stepped forward in faith, the more he heard God's reassuring voice, speaking through His Holy Spirit with a sense of consolation.

Here, Moses listened, and God entrusted Him with leading the people out of Egypt. Will you aspire to listen to God and be faithful to Him?

3. Moses Questions and Prays Through God's Empowerment

In Exodus 4:1–17 we see that Moses struggles as he processes the task ahead. Moses asks (v1), "What if they do not believe or listen to me?" Is this our reaction sometime: What if people make fun of or ridicule me? This is really honest and something that would happen to most of us. God responds by equipping Moses in three different ways: a staff, a cloak and a brother to work with. Be alert and ready for God to use what is before us to do glorious things. However, when Moses looked for excuses, God rebuked him again, giving him Aaron, who could speak well.

God was generous in giving Moses both miraculous powers but also allowing for practical support in having Aaron by his side. However, interestingly, having Aaron was not God's original intention. Aaron's help would also lead to a thorn in Moses' side as he would later build the Golden Calf and challenge Moses' leadership. When God speaks to us, it is best to follow His provisions. God wanted to work directly with Moses so that Moses would see the power of God through him. He did not need another speaker; God would lead Him. He needed faith not to be afraid. Moses questioned God's equipping, but God was patient, kind and gentle. Yet, the second-best decisions led to second-best outcomes. Take God at His word the first time around. He is there – He wants to equip you for the tasks. He calls you with provisions, with skills to put your hand to and with brothers around you too. What was the last thing God told you to do? Have you done it?

God had met Moses in the wilderness at the burning bush, revealed His plans and empowered him to make a difference. Exodus 4:21, "The Lord said to Moses, 'When you return to Egypt, see that you perform before Pharaoh all the wonders I have given you the power to do.'" God first spoke to Aaron and drew him into the wilderness, where he met Moses (v27). He spoke on his behalf to the Israelites as Moses performed signs and wonders, no doubt using the sign of his hand in the cloak. Like Aaron, God brings people across our paths at the perfect times. We can trust Him to do this; people can be a massive blessing.

In Exodus 5, Moses met Pharoah to say, "This is what the Lord, the God of Israel, says: 'Let my people go, so that they may hold a festival to Me in the wilderness.'" Watch Pharaoh's reaction. How does it compare to Moses' response to God's voice? Does he take a further look, acknowledge God is greater and say, "Here I am, Lord"? It is a contrast. In verse two, "Pharaoh said, 'Who is the Lord, that I should obey Him and let Israel go? I do not know the Lord and will not let Israel go.'" Pharoah's heart was hardened towards God. Where is your heart? Will you react in prayer to take a further look, listen and offer yourself when He speaks? Or will you harden your heart questioning His character and jurisdiction in your life and say that you'd rather not know Him? These are life's crucial choices. These are the sliding door moments. God gives us so many chances to choose Him. Look at Pharaoh: he had ten plagues and more than ten opportunities to choose God and turn to follow Him, but he rejected God as Lord in his life.

The more Moses followed God, the more aspiration his faith journey had. The closer we are to our Saviour, the more we think as He does, the more we are transformed into His likeness and the more likely we are to hear that reminding voice in our hearts. Moses went on to use his staff in Exodus 7, turning it into a snake; Pharaoh's magicians turned theirs into snakes, too, but Moses' snake ate theirs. We will encounter challenges as we follow God. Will we give up? Or will we trust that God's plans will eat the enemies for breakfast? To trust God with our lives requires steps of faith. This may often mean that things will turn out differently from what we expect. However, although it can appear dangerous – the safest place is in His hands. Let's pray, "Lord, make me braver to do Your will. Amen."

Summary

God gave Moses free will to choose to follow in the aspiration of faith or not. God gives you and me choices, too. How will we respond? Our reactions are crucial to us and those around us. Pharoah's response was to be unwilling to compromise, resistant to change and to be unfaithful in listening to God, leading to giant consequences and death. Don't be like him. After crossing the Red Sea, the Israelites rejected God when they were nearly at the Promised Land. This meant that God kept almost an entire generation in the wilderness for forty years. Why? Because He gives us choices. Do you want to live in the wilderness of life or the Promised Land?

To do this, we will face challenging steps of faith. We will require God's courage to say "yes" to the aspiration of His calling. Decide today to keep an open heart, take a further look, listen to God, and say "Here am I. I'm ready to follow You." Psalm 16:11 says, "You make known to me the path of life; You will fill me with joy in Your presence, with eternal pleasures at Your right hand." God has exciting plans for each of us. He wants to show us His plans, fill us with joy as we walk in them and bring us into the pleasures of eternity with Him. We all have challenges and unique roads to navigate, but God builds His church, and as we know from Ephesians 2, God has plans prepared in advance for us to do. If we listen, He will equip and empower us to follow. So, will we listen like Moses or shy away? Will we question God in setbacks or resist Him like Pharoah? Will we pray and remember or grumble and reject Him? Choose to follow Him in faith, humbly learn from any mistakes made, and we can then be assured of God's ongoing Fatherly love. Following God's call is the heart of the ultimate aspiration.

JOE LOWTHER

PART THREE
| COMPASSION |

JOE LOWTHER

Chapter 5
Compassion: KICK's Story

Why is compassion important? Why is compassion needed? Why is it valued at KICK? How we treat, react and respond to young people must be motivated by compassion. Our mission is to transform young people's lives with God's love. Compassion is key. Young people have gone through so much and face many present dangers. Seventy-five percent of psychiatric problems start in adolescence, and in the last three years post-COVID, CAMHS (Children and Adolescent Mental Health Services) referrals have increased by eighty-five percent. Four million children in the UK now will grow up in lone-parent families[12] and UNICEF states that being fatherless is one of the four pillars of global poverty. Children and young people need surrogate fathers and advocates to address these challenges. It is heart breaking to hear that the top question surveyed by young people post-pandemic was, "Will everything be OK?"[13] The problems faced are not just personal but social, too. The Children's Commissioner stated that "closing of schools during lockdown has had an enormous impact on children's holistic wellbeing." In addition, the "reduction in physical activity saw children become more withdrawn and suffer in isolation, which saw their confidence levels fall."[14] This has led to widespread school absenteeism post-COVID, which has led to more isolated children, with one in four school children now "persistently absent".[15] Children and young people need change motivated by compassion more than ever.

Compassion is valued deeply by God. He introduces Himself to Moses, saying, "I am compassionate" in Exodus 22:27, and it is this example we look to follow at KICK. The Psalmist says, "The Lord is compassionate and gracious, slow to anger, abounding in love" (Psalm 103:8). From this, we aim to be patient and generous to our young people. Jesus gave young people quality time and was aware of their vulnerabilities, warning those who abuse power (Mark 9:35–37). Jesus stood up for young people, aware that they can often be disempowered in society, challenging leaders not to hinder "the little children" (Mark 10:14–16; Luke 18:16). Jesus showed great compassion to children as in the example of the possessed boy whom He personally freed (Mark 9:14–29). God looks to have compassion on people as a father would his children, inspiring us in how we treat others (Psalm 103:13, Isaiah 49:15). Compassion is expressed in kindness during grief and when showing mercy (Isaiah 63:7, Lamentations 3:32, Zechariah 7:9). Jesus, as our example, had compassion on the many, expressed compassion for those in need and spoke of having compassion on one lost sheep even if he already had ninety-nine others (Matthew 14:14, Mark 8:2, Luke 15:3-7). Christians are called to "clothe yourselves with compassion, kindness, humility, gentleness and patience" (Colossians 3:12). Therefore, to imbue our work with compassion, we must wrap ourselves in it too.

1. Responding to Change

Trustee, Mike Wakeham, was a Magistrate in 2005 and sat in the youth court. He reflected, "We regularly had discussions on the reasons youths got themselves into trouble with the law and concluded there was no single reason — low self-esteem, no good role models in their lives, mixing with the wrong crowd, peer pressure, family background, local environment are but a few. When I looked at KICK's remit for changing lives, it mirrored much of my experience in court. I was very attracted to the KICK ethos, particularly with the added dimension of spreading the word of God. It was a rewarding time as we multiplied, and everyone was incredibly supportive. In April 2007, we ran our first football tournament at Croydon High School, attracting thirty teams from twelve churches." Compassion motivated a reaction.

2. Can You Be My Daddy?

When conducting a lunchtime club in Heathfield Juniors, Simon James, our Head of Mentoring, was approached by an eight-year-old girl. She asked, "Will you mentor me?" He replied, "I'd love to, but I work from the caseload the school gives me." She took time to think through her response and said, "Alright, well, would you become my daddy?" She had never known her father, had no brothers and had not yet had male teachers in her school. Children in our society face many challenges and need good role models wherever we can provide them. This challenged our ignorance that it was only boys who needed male role models. Girls do, too, and as a result, this motivated us to develop and grow our mentoring provision.

3. Christmas Presents

During the Cost-of-Living Crisis, we provided KICK Holiday Camps in the community of Richmond. You'd assume that there are only affluent families there. Still, an absence of services means that for those who are disadvantaged, there is little help they receive from the local authority. We worked with a local grant funding organisation that covered a cohort of children free of charge. One of these parents approached us and said, "We can't afford Christmas presents this year. I know the KICK Camp is fully funded, but would you mind if we told the kids that the KICK Camp is their Christmas present?" Of course, this was fine. Their economic deprivation was obvious, and we were proud to be able to host these young people and support these families. Not to mention anything to the children, we were able to show compassion through dignity.

4. The Release of Forgiveness

Coach Stuart Kennett gave nine years of his career to KICK and was a fantastic role model to the young people. In his interview to join KICK, he famously said, "I don't even like football, but I'd do plant-potting if it helped introduce young people to Jesus." Stuart reflected, "In primary school in Penge, I had the privilege of taking lessons, attending regular assemblies and mentoring a select number of children. The assemblies gave me the opportunity to creatively – with games and stories – expand on the values underpinning all that KICK is built on to introduce how much God loves them. On one occasion, the assembly was about forgiveness and having a fresh start. We focused on the fact that forgiveness is just as much about releasing and freeing ourselves from anger and resentment as the person we seek to forgive. God always offers us a fresh start because God is Love. Seeing some children attempt to forgive during our sessions, particularly aggressive and competitive football games (!), was great! It was so encouraging to see that some of the children I taught and mentored then went on to join their local church's KICK Academy, growing in their understanding and faith of what it means to be loved by God and follow Jesus!"

5. The Bridge

One of our mentors, Davey Murphy, worked with a mentee who had existential depression. This meant she was depressed about the existence of life. It took time to build trust, but once this was established from a place of compassion, she opened up to Davey that she had left her house at midnight, gone to a bridge overlooking a dual carriageway to throw herself off, got cold feet and went home. She had been suicidal for six months, and this was the first person she had told. Davey was able to affirm her value and work with the school to make sure there was an entire team to support her when she got home that day. When they next met, Davey was nervous about how she would react that he had had to escalate this situation, but she thanked him. She said, "That was the first time in my life I knew someone cared that I was alive." Over the next eighteen months, Davey continued to mentor her through to the end of her GCSEs. In their final mentoring session, she wrote him a card which said, "Thank you for giving me a reason to live." It is not always that one's work is life or death, but that day, we were reminded that at KICK, sometimes our work is a matter of life and death.

6. Church Compassion

The brilliant Trevor and Kate Patterson were essential in creating KICK when we were founded. Kate Patterson shares her experiences motivated by compassion, "When KICK started, we were praying about how our church could reach out to the community and not be stuck in the building. When it all began, my husband, Trevor, was the Vicar of Holy Trinity Richmond. He was also an avid football fan who never quite grew out of falling asleep dreaming of scoring a Premiership goal. I remember his excitement when he came home from dreaming about KICK, beginning with Tom Rutter, our first KICK coach! Over the years, we saw KICK's impact on many lives and our church community. I loved how it drew in families from different classes and ethnic and religious backgrounds. As sport and faith in Jesus can do, it brought us all together. We saw lives changed, and KICK was an important part of that.

"The church had a ministry to vulnerable families. It was a brilliant resource for those without positive role models at home. I can think of one family where there had been generations of addiction and the problems that go with it. The kids found a regular, safe place to attend KICK. That value is not to be underestimated because they desperately needed consistent, hope-filled input. They loved football, which was a guaranteed way to connect with them. All of them eventually got baptised in their late teens and have broken the cycle of addiction. KICK blessed not only our church community but also our own family. Our three sons grew up turning up to church in a football strip and then going straight from a service to a match. They discovered that God isn't only in church and can even be found on a football field! I will always be grateful for that and the brilliant friend and role model they found in Tom. Over the years before he died, Trevor was utterly behind the vision of KICK – as a Vicar, as a Trustee and as a dad of attendees. I know he would have joined me in being thrilled to see the charity grow from strength to strength, reaching many and fulfilling the vision to transform lives."

7. Christ Central KICK Academy

I met with a church in Penge before a new KICK Academy training day. The church leader said that the previous Sunday, they had played a kickabout with some of the lads and dads, and they had been struck that some of the kids from a local estate had come out and asked to play. Meeting with me, Glen said I can see how this can work. We want to do it now. He was so captivated by the idea of a KICK Academy that he sent a team to the KICK Academy training day the following morning. The wonderful Becci Lee and Alistair Park became coaches who not only worked for KICK but also volunteered to run their church KICK Academy. A month later, we distributed flyers to two local Primary schools the week before the KICK Academy launched. In week one, twenty-four kids came; in week two, thirty-two kids; in week three, thirty-six kids. They had to cap the KICK Academy at seventy-two kids. Towards the end of the term, a single mother with five kids came down and asked, "Why are you doing this? We pay £12 a term, but do you buy a Capri Sun and a Mars Bar for each kid weekly? What's in it for you?" They shared with her the Gospel, and she gave her life to the Lord at the side of the pitch. She was baptised the following December and became a part of the local church with her family: a chance to transform young people's and mum's lives.

8. Transition to Transformation

Jonathan Sanders, one of our mentors, worked with a learner who had a complicated home life at a primary school. Things improved, but we were concerned that our engagement would end as he graduated from secondary school. By God's grace, he progressed to another secondary school where we provided Chaplaincy. Familiar with KICK, he started to come to a Christian Union there, took an Alpha for Schools course and gave his life to God. He began engaging in youth work at Holy Trinity Richmond Church. He even invited four new friends to the next Alpha for Schools course. He was an excellent example of personal, social and spiritual transformation. Jonathan recalled, "It was such a joy to work at KICK and be a part of something extraordinary. I have seen the incredible work that KICK has done to transform young people's lives. Two years later, I bumped into him, and he said, 'I'm the student that you mentored.' It was then that he said he was really enjoying secondary school and that the themes and space the mentoring sessions provided were so helpful for him. Stories like this are just an example of KICK's role in providing young people in schools across the country joy in the present and hope for the future."

9. Colourful Emotions

Moved by compassion, mentor PK observed, "A boy struggled to communicate his emotions. I believe God allowed me to break down the emotions in his life. I asked him to explain how he felt through colours or pictures when angry. He said black and red. Red for anger and black for confusion. He said black because he felt like a cloud around his head. On my way home, I prayed for him and I felt God say that we would change the colours that he specifically sees. It wasn't instant, but he began sharing more of his emotions over time. The boy was like a hedgehog, bottling up his emotions and resisting talking about them. Still, it got to the point that when that happened, he would find me to share when he was feeling low. Seeing God using us as a vessel to bring change and light to young people's lives was encouraging. I now mentor his sister. She is like a rhino and over-expressive, but they both have the same trigger. Anytime they don't feel perfect, they retreat or erupt. Schools can be an environment where they fail and feel like failure. I have been able to build her self-esteem. Thanks be to God because she now sees that she is valued regardless of results."

10. Space to Grieve

KICK Chaplain Simon Gee reflects, "A year seven pupil was new to secondary school and adjusting to the greater independence required when he discovered that his favourite primary school teacher had died suddenly in his mid-thirties due to COVID-19. Although no longer at the school, his teacher had been very kind and fun, greatly impacting this pupil during his formative years. To lose a constant in his life and experience loss for the first time at such a transitional stage was very hard. While meeting him as chaplain, we saw many sad emotions and tears, and he processed his feelings. We got him a time-out card so he could leave lessons and come and chat if they became too much for him to handle. After a few weeks, the sessions, chats and prayers helped him feel better about himself. They gave him a more positive school experience. This provided him with a caring adult when he had lost his."

Summary

"People don't care how much you know until they know how much you care" – Theodore Roosevelt

Our objective is to deliver services infused with compassion that motivate us to empathise, engage and serve young people. Knowing they have implicit value, we seek to love them with compassion, requiring our whole heart, soul, and strength, which we will reflect on in the next chapter.

JOE LOWTHER

Chapter 6
Compassion: Spiritual Application

Compassion is a crucial aspect of love in the Bible. How to love is well summed up in Deuteronomy as Moses preached his last sermon to remind the next generation to remain faithful to God before they entered the Promised Land. Moses said in Deuteronomy 6:4–5, "Hear, O Israel: The Lord our God, the Lord is one. Love the Lord your God with all your heart and with all your soul and with all your strength." A dive into this presents an opportunity to understand how to be compassionate.

1. Heart, Soul and Strength

Heart, soul, and strength are distinct and also interrelated. The Bible references the heart in matters of belief, passion, conscience, character, understanding, intention and desire. So, when we think of heart, we now think of intent. While the term "soul" does include emotional qualities, it is more deep-seated bedrock feelings that intensely affect our sense of life or self. Our strength is our ability, agency or power to love God. This may even include all of one's estate: possessions, health and household – so nothing is left outside the realm of loving God with our "all." These are the three elements with which Moses calls us to love God.

The Jewish people revere Deuteronomy 6:4–9 as their "Shema Yisrael" and Jesus takes this up in a summary of the greatest commandments in the three synoptic

Gospels.[16] We can faithfully re-articulate Deuteronomy 6 as "love God with all that you can (heart); all that you are (soul), and all that you have (strength)." The Bible sets "loving God" in the context of an exhortation: it becomes galvanising (strength) for not only how we feel about God (heart) but also inspires our desires for Him (soul). Loving God can motivate our every decision and empower our very lives. Therefore, we can love God with all we have because He cleanses and enables us. Following God and loving Him with all our heart, soul and strength is what God desires, and it involves action. We love God with all our hearts when we love Him alone. We love God with all our souls when we find our satisfaction in Him more than any other person or thing. We love God with all our strength when we obey Him and persevere in the face of every trial.

2. Independent or Interrelated

It can be confusing to dissect these elements. Still, we can become confident they are interrelated, and we should understand them individually. The collective meaning is the more profound lesson. We are not to love God with only part of ourselves but to consider each thought, feeling and action in light of our will to honour Him. We are to pursue our love for Him in every aspect of daily life with all that we are. The important thing is not a distinction between the various parts but their unity, interdependence and integration. Rather than just the more Greek thinking of distinction or tripartite psychology, the emphasis is on loving and obeying with "everything we've got." 2 Kings 23:25 shows a practical example, "Neither before nor after Josiah was there a king like him who turned to the Lord as he did – with all his heart and with all his soul and with all his strength, by all the Law of Moses." Can we be more like Josiah as we love God? Where do we need to get right with God today? In what ways can we repledge ourselves to a covenantal relationship with God? How can we rely more on His strength to accomplish this? This requires our heart, soul and strength to do this. In understanding the first commandment, we can consider what Jesus meant by the second commandment summary: love your neighbour as yourself. We are to love God with all our heart, soul, and strength – but to love our neighbour too. We will look at Luke 10 and the context around the summary of the call to love our neighbour.

3. Love Your Close Neighbour

The context to Jesus' summary of these commandments is Luke 10:1–24. Jesus sent out the seventy-two disciples in pairs (v1) on potentially dangerous missions to share the Good News of the Messiah's arrival. We see in verse two that Jesus challenges them to pray for more workers instead of a plentiful harvest. There are few workers, so ask God to send them. There is an urgency and a danger to this mission that Jesus highlights in verse three to four. "Go!" Jesus exclaims, calling them to drop everything and realise that they would be lambs among wolves. The mission that God sends His followers on can be dangerous so show compassion and love one another.

Jesus' reaction when "the seventy-two" returned home safely was to rejoice with love (v17–19), not in the power they had seen outworked, but in the reality that their names were written in heaven. This reality of the gift of eternal life is a shared point of worship for those who have chosen to follow Jesus today. Praise the Lord. Celebrating this truth and encouraging one another to press on towards the unseen rather than just the seen, is essential as we love our neighbours in our context. In verse twenty-one, Jesus worships the Father and becomes joyful as He sees the Holy Spirit work in their lives. We can marvel at the Glorious Father still at work in His followers today.

In verse twenty-four, many prophets and kings wanted to see what had been revealed to Christians but could not. We, as God's family, have received revelation fit for kings. We are unbelievably blessed that Jesus has chosen to reveal Himself to us and that we have the entire canon of Scripture. Let this fuel our compassion and love for one another as fellow heirs to the Kingdom of Heaven. The love of God has no favourites. Each son and daughter of God is a prince and princess for eternity. We need not be jealous of fellow heirs but instead champion each other. Remember King Saul's son, Prince Jonathan who although he was the biological heir to the throne, fought to save David's life at the risk of his own. He believed in faith that David would one day be king instead of himself and in humility, he honoured his friend. We should have Prince Jonathan's attitude.

To whom are you being asked to show compassion? What relationships do you need to get right? Where are you showing love where it's bearing fruit? Where might God be leading you to replicate that? Who loves well whom you admire, and what can you borrow to better impact your close relationships? Love your close neighbours well.

4. Love Your Stranger Neighbour

In loving our neighbour, this might be to show compassion to someone we doesn't even know, as we see in Luke 10:5–16. In verse five Jesus instructs His disciples to look for people of peace in new locations. God will lead them to go to strangers to share the Good News (v6–7), stay where they are welcomed (v8) and work as a blessing for their benefit, healing the sick. In mission, God calls us to be a blessing to others whom He knows inside out, but often whom we are unfamiliar with. However, in v10–16, when they are not welcomed, they are directed to keep moving, entrusting the consequences to the Lord.

We will meet different strangers in our lives. Do we have an intent to show compassion and share Jesus with them? In 2023, at the Youth for Christ Conference in Blackpool, I walked down the pier with KICK Chaplain Samuel. He is an evangelist, and as we walked, he shared the Gospel with three different people walking their dogs. One he had a five-minute conversation with, but two others he just said, "Do you know that Jesus loves you? Please reflect on this and consider Him in your heart." We might not be evangelists, but we have all been called to be witnesses, to be ready and to be available, and to seek opportunities to share our hope in Jesus. Let's be willing and prepared to share Him. You never know. It might be easier than to share with those with whom we have a long-term relationship. Let's look for opportunities which the Holy Spirit presents. This is the same Holy Spirit which led Jesus to the man at the pool in Bethsaida in John 5 to bring healing and set him free. Do we suspect that the Holy Spirit does not want to guide us to bring healing? Sometimes, we can feel that way, but no – let's be ready to share and give hope to others as the seventy-two were and as we have the same Holy Spirit guiding our lives.

How can we be more ready to meet new people? What might you say? Are you praying for the Holy Spirit to guide you to meet others you don't know and show kindness? Don't be foolish, but don't hide the Good News that you now know. Be ready and ask God to lead you to show compassion to strangers with acts worthy of the loving Father and sacrificial Son.

5. Love Your Enemy Neighbour

The third part is for us to consider showing compassion to our enemy. Jesus said in John 15:13, "Greater love has no one other than this: to lay down one's life for one's friends." We are to be ready to sacrifice ourselves for our friends, but Jesus goes further, as we see in Romans 5:6–8. Paul the Apostle underlines, "You see, at just the right time, when we were still powerless, Christ died for the ungodly. Very rarely will anyone die for a righteous person, though for a good person, someone might possibly dare to die. But God demonstrates His love for us in this: While we were still sinners, Christ died for us." Jesus died for the Disciples on the Cross as His friends and remember each disciple deserted Him in some way, particularly painfully as with Peter. But Jesus also died for His enemies. Whilst we were still sinners, Christ died for us. Jesus leads by example in His love for us. He gave His life not only for His friends but those who hated Him. He even cried out for His executioners at the Cross: "Father, forgive them for they know not what they do" (Luke 23:34). This is unreal compassion for even His murderers.

So, back in Luke 10:25–37, Jesus is questioned about how to inherit eternal life. Still, He responds with a question, "What is written in the Law? How do you read it?" The Priest replies (v27), "'Love the Lord your God with all your heart and with all your soul and with all your strength and with all your mind' and 'Love your neighbour as yourself.'" Jesus validates this correct response but extends the boundaries of who our neighbour is, introducing the Parable of the Good Samaritan.

After the attack, the man from Jerusalem was twice passed by Jewish leaders, by a Priest and then by a Levite. The two people who would have been expected to show compassion left him for dead. Ouch. However, in verse thirty-three, a Samaritan, an enemy of the Jewish people, took pity and showed love. When we encounter those different from us, those we disagree with and those who might have caused us pain as our enemies, will we see those very people when they are in pain and show love? How will we operate if we see people with distinctly alternative ideological beliefs or from different religious convictions? How would we love them? We are directed to be prepared to care for them. In verse thirty-four, the Samaritan went to him and showed compassion. Will we be ready to give time and be a part of bandaging people's wounds? Will we invest time and money as the Samaritan did to pour out oil and wine to bring someone through a painful situation? Are we inspired by the love of Christ within us to use our vehicles, pay for the board for others and spend time caring for those we don't naturally care for? If not, will we be prepared to pray and ask God to change our hearts, to beat in harmony with His for others?

The Good Samaritan is a parable that Jesus uses to show His love for us. Remember, we were enemies of God, but He made a decision of the heart, preserved through the pain, and died to save us. Jesus challenges us to follow His example to love those with whom we don't have things in common and show comfort in pain, as He says in verse thirty-seven, "Go and do likewise." Loving our neighbour is not always about those we like or people we don't know; it can be those we dislike. The challenges of the Lord Jesus are not always easy to follow, but the narrow path. Let's pray and ask the Lord to prepare our hearts, for the Holy Spirit to direct us and be led by Christ's example of love, to follow the narrow paths as we love our neighbours.

It is instructive to reflect on the final verses of Luke 10:38–42, on Mary and Martha's example. We have access to Jesus through the Holy Spirit, and this is an excellent example of how we should balance these top two commandments. We must love one another practically but not at the expense of time with the Father. Martha was rebuked by the Lord even though she was working hard like the Good Samaritan – this was because it was at the expense of time with the Lord.

Summary

Therefore, let us love God with all that we can (heart), all that we are (soul), and all that we have (strength), and love our neighbour whether they are close to us, unknown to us or even those we know we don't like. Keep your approach to compassion in that priority order, remembering that these are two priorities that Jesus says are faith in action and enabling us to inherit eternal life. In putting God first, we can love others effectively. Jesus has won the battle at the Cross, and we are justified by His sacrifice, sanctified through obedience towards Him. We will be glorified with Him in eternal life. Let's start by loving Him and showing compassion to others as He guides us.

JOE LOWTHER

PART FOUR
| EXCELLENCE |

JOE LOWTHER

Chapter 7
Excellence: KICK's Story

At KICK, we want to develop innovative new provision to meet needs and inspire young people. Studies have shown that Physical Education is neglected[17] and teachers are not confident in delivering it.[18] Even Ofsted[19] has reported that there is "insufficient ambition in UK Physical Education." Physical Education can play a vital role in connecting important ideas about health to physical activity. Young people need role models passionate about sport or dance who can coach with joy. Delivering services with excellence is vital for KICK's credibility in schools, the integrity of our offer and the benefit of young people.

This value is inspired by our Christian ethos. At the start of all things, we see that God is a God of excellence as the Bible states that, "God saw all that He had made, and it was very good" (Genesis 1:31). Jesus Christ was an excellent teacher whose teaching remains spoken of today, which is a clear affirmation of what we do as we educate our young people (Mark 10:1). Furthermore, He was relevant in the way He taught using parables and metaphors to unlock hearts and minds. Jesus was an outstanding leader, developing a team with the disciples, a wider team with the seventy-two, that saw many follow Him (Luke 5:27-28). Jesus knew His task and stuck at it, though it had a cost, as He gave Himself for the cause (Galatians 2:20). This example of Jesus inspires us to give our all at KICK to the young people we work with. God challenges Christians to serve faithfully and to have a standing of excellence (1 Timothy 3:13).

The Bible urges Christians to focus on excellence when it says, "Whatever is true, whatever is noble, whatever is right, whatever is pure, whatever is lovely, whatever is admirable – if anything is excellent or praiseworthy – think about such things" (Philippians 4:8). We believe that it is right to devote ourselves to doing what is good (Titus 3:8) and thus to deliver with excellence.

1. Forty Parables in the Bible

When we launched our dance provision, a primary school approached us because of the way we could help develop schools' Christian distinctiveness. As a single-form entry Church of England Primary School in North London, the school had not only an Ofsted Inspection but also a SIAMS Inspection. This reviewed the quality of the Christian Character of the school. The headteacher confided in me that they had achieved "outstanding" on the previous framework but were due for a new inspection, and they hadn't changed much since the last inspection. Additionally, the goalposts had changed with an updated framework, and the school now needed to get an "excellent" to keep par with the previous grade. Could KICK help develop the Christian distinctiveness further? Absolutely, we said. We'd love to investigate this. We brainstormed and developed a bespoke Scheme of Work based around the forty parables in the Bible, one for every Academic week of the year, building a dance move connected to that parable, through to a performance piece of the Parables of the Sower, Lost

Sheep and Good Samaritan. We had a unique opportunity to share the words of Jesus with the young people through dance. I visited the performance piece, and it was moving to see the learners perform this piece of musical theatre, teaching their parents and carers the parables of Christ. Rachel Hollings recalled, "We were backstage waiting to go on, and one of the girls turns around and says, 'We are so nervous. Can we even do this?' Then she asked if I could pray for them all. They held hands and waited for me to pray. It was a beautiful moment where I just took a second and thought, 'Wow, what a privilege I have right now to encourage and ask Jesus to be with them.' Her hope and ambition not to give up was inspiring, and they absolutely smashed that performance." A piece of intentional mission delivered with excellence.

2. Smart Resources

St Michaels Church in Southfields approached KICK with a proposal – they wanted to employ their intern as a youth worker at their church, and would KICK consider employing this intern part-time to work as a KICK coach? We interviewed Robbie Smart and were delighted to bring him on board two days per week with KICK whilst he worked three days with the church. Robbie was brilliant as he engaged in the St Michael's Church youthwork. We trained him to launch the St Michaels KICK Academy, and then we placed him at the local St Michaels CE Primary School. This was a clear example of an intentional mission, and Robbie delivered excellent work. This led to many young people feeling freer to transition between school and the church. There was a big field overseen by the church and opposite the school. Robbie welcomed kids he saw in the school and saw them engaged with the KICK Academy. Parents could see KICK in the school and then KICK in the community; they fed back and felt more at ease sending their kids to the church. Today, we have KICK Academies staffed with excellent volunteers such as teenagers hoping to develop their CVs, ninety-year-old ladies who make tea and coffees who gossip the Gospel at the side of the pitch, determined mums, passionate grandpas, all shapes and sizes. As the Apostle Paul says in 1 Corinthians 9: 22, "I have become all things to all people so that by all possible means I might save some."

3. Values-Driven Coaching

KICK Quality Manager Andy Dutton reflects, "At KICK, we feel very privileged to share the Bible in a way that feels both relevant and exciting, especially to those from unchurched backgrounds. Initially, it felt like the church had left the building, but taking it into schools felt like unchartered territory. We developed a values-driven approach to coaching, which builds on the Fruits of the Spirit. The practical outworking of this was so exciting to see.

"We would play games with the children where there was a real jeopardy of losing the game or being out and having them referee their own performance with the value of Integrity and the motto, 'Do the right thing, even if nobody is watching.' It was lovely to see children beginning to understand that sport was one place where emotions and frustrations would run high. Still, they could apply 'self-control' to their performance and avoid conflict. We would see young people 'compassionately' picking their opponent up off the floor after a heavy tackle in rugby or displaying 'kindness' when someone hadn't been picked for a team. Our learners often found some of the sports difficult to learn but remained 'faithful' to their learning and demonstrated 'perseverance' to overcome challenges. We began to see leaders emerge, learning to be 'patient' with their teammates and peers of lower ability and display 'gentleness' in communicating feedback.

We used sport to emulate life's tensions, frustrations and stresses and a battleground of conflicting emotions. Through this, we demonstrated the need for sharing KICK values in day-to-day life. A learner who would regularly lash out at playtime would come to know how they could develop 'self-control' in their life and avoid getting in trouble; a learner who would regularly give up on their Maths work would now 'persevere' to overcome the challenge because they had done the same in dance. For me, that privilege that I felt when I started at KICK has never changed. I couldn't care less whether they could kick a ball any better because of me. Still, I absolutely care that they grow up to be good human beings with the knowledge of how to demonstrate love to others. Sport is a wonderful opportunity to communicate key values and messages of hope."

4. Cerebal Palsy: Perseverance

In the West Midlands, coach Rob Curtis mentored a year ten girl who suffered with cerebral palsy. She suffered from anxiety and had to cope with extreme pain in her legs daily due to her condition. As part of Rob's mentoring sessions, he talked through the daily challenges that led to her school life, ranging from academic struggles to coping with pain levels to managing relationships with staff. This winter, she will complete her Year Ten mock exams, a work experience placement and an operation in mid-February. This is understandably causing her high levels of anxiety and worry. Hence, they discussed coping mechanisms to calm her and reflected on examples of where she has succeeded. Rob reports, "Since mentoring, the results have been a resilient individual, willing to give her everything to overcome the barriers in her life." Rob's impact on this young person's life gave her the confidence to press on. This story demonstrates the importance of excellent mentoring, which has improved attendance and conduct at school and a new willingness to persevere through her challenges.

5. The Lost Art of Intercessory Prayer

In 2016, Neil O'Boyle shared a challenge at the Youth for Christ Conference, saying that he felt the UK had lost the art of intercession. Neil had been abroad for over a decade on an international mission in the Middle East, and he identified a change in people's ability to intercede. He asserted, "If mission truly belongs to God, then it is imperative to focus and listen to God. Prayer must not just be about arts and craft but about hearing His voice and interceding on other peoples' behalf." At Board level it got us thinking about what intercessory prayer means. There were a few vague answers, but we decided to dig deeper and ensure clarity. We first defined that personal prayer is broken down into three areas in Philippians 4:6–7: prayer (an outpouring of your heart), petition (requests) and thanksgiving (remembering that every good gift in our lives comes from the Lord). Intercession is about praying on others' behalf. In the Old Testament, there are three great examples: Abraham, Samuel and Daniel; and in the New Testament, Jesus brilliantly prays for Himself for the benefit of His followers, then intercedes for His disciples and finally for the whole world of believers.

We see in Romans 8:34 that Jesus "was raised to life – is at the right hand of God and is also interceding for us" today. We felt stirred to intercede for young people at KICK. In addition, the following is a list of those for whom we are to offer intercessory prayers: all in authority (1 Timothy 2:2), church leaders (Philippians 1:19), Jerusalem (Psalm 122:6), friends (Job 42:8), fellow countrymen (Romans 10:1), the sick (James 5:14), enemies (Jeremiah 29:7), those who persecute us (Matthew 5:44), those who forsake us (2 Timothy 4:16) and all men (1 Timothy 2:1). Intercession is prayer that pleads with God for your needs and the needs of others, but it is also much more than that. Intercession involves taking hold of God's will and refusing to let go until His will comes to pass. We felt challenged to be ready to go deeper, be more directed and have a cutting edge in intercession. This led to creating a weekly prayer meeting and 24/1 prayer day to intercede for our young people at KICK.

6. Not just Sport Specialists Needed

James Lowther, founding trustee at KICK, recalls, "Rev. Trevor Patterson introduced me to Tom Rutter and his vision for KICK in 2003. Barry Mason of Youth for Christ challenged us as the early trustees to take the administrative workload off Tom to free him up to work with young people. I used my accountancy training to register the charity, do the bookkeeping and deal with The Charity Commission, Companies House and HMRC. It has been my joy to give thousands of hours of my time during the first twenty years of KICK, as I knew I could be part of seeing Christians connect with young people.

"Sadly, so few young people in Britain today know Christ. Sunday schools were widely attended in the first half of the twentieth century. Thomas Laqueur estimated that there were approximately 5,952,431 children enrolled in schools in 1901, 6,178,827 in 1906, and 6,129,496 in 1911. In 2000, it was estimated that fewer than ten per cent of children attended Sunday school.[20] I was excited that KICK would be encouraging churches to run football alongside church and that we would be taking our Christian coaches into schools: whilst few children attend church, almost all of them are to be found in schools.

"Our focus was football initially, but I remember one trustee meeting when we were wondering if we should consider training coaches in other sports. My response was, 'If it gives us the opportunity to communicate Jesus to young people, I don't mind if we offer tiddlywinks!'

"There were some financial challenges in the early years, but we all trusted God and overcame them. Having offered free coaching to our first schools, we were delighted that schools were willing to pay us for this! The government's introduction in 2005 of PPA (a half-day free for each primary school teacher for planning, preparation, and assessment) opened a door for KICK, as schools employed us to fill the gap. What a delight to sense that we were part of something significant and that God was leading and blessing us. The adventure continues!"

This shows that all skills, not just those of the coaches, were required for the mission. Give what you can to make a difference.

7. Female Role Models

Physical activity has much to offer everyone, particularly for girls. The 'Teenage Girls and Sport Report' found playing sport could boost girls' happiness and confidence. Girls who didn't play sport were four times more likely to have low body confidence and lower wellbeing ratings than their sport-playing peers. However, sadly, there are many barriers which prevent girls' engagement, such as body image and puberty. Stephanie Hilborne[21] said, "Girls losing sport from their lives during these formative years equates to a loss of joy as well as good lifelong health." We must do more, or we face a generational missed opportunity. I want to introduce you to coach Zoe Cross. She was a former Chelsea footballer who bravely decided to transition to sports coaching and mentoring with girls. This year, Zoe has mentored challenging children, coached all types of sports in schools and brilliantly led physical rehabilitation at an alternative provision that provides education for girls with complex mental and physical health needs. Zoe is an excellent role model for girls. We need more female role models and to hear their stories to give girls someone to chase for engagement in sport.

8. Climbing the Walls to Play Sport

Former Quality Manager Hans Sims said, "I often visually picture kids from the local estate climbing over the walls to get to the Saturday Spring Park KICK Academy at the local school playing fields. Many of them were from unchurched families, and it was wonderful to see the interest the children had in both the football training, the matches and the 'God slot.'" It was very much like the story of how those friends broke off the roof to get the paralysed man to Jesus to be healed. That desire was there for the kids to get them to sport. "Interestingly, a few have reached out in recent years to say how much they valued the time at the KICK Academy and its positive impact on their lives." This was personified by Dan, who came to the Spring Park KICK Academy and went on to become a youth player for Crystal Palace Football Club. After being released from Crystal Palace, Dan shared his time between semi-professional football and coaching at KICK, displaying his personal commitment to excellence by giving back to his community.

Summary

In seeking to be excellent in our service provision for the sake of young people's personal, social and spiritual challenges, we are motivated by our Christian ethos – to follow Jesus' example in the way He loved young people and was relevant in the way He communicated with them. Our incredible coaches, mentors and chaplains, led by brilliant managers, aim to provide a credible service that is impactful and transformative. In addition, we know that our mission is inspired by God's involvement in our work. To be excellent, we need to pray for His engagement.

JOE LOWTHER

Chapter 8
Excellence: Spiritual Application

To serve with excellence, we need to be connected to the Author and Perfector of our faith. This means we need to pray to operate with accuracy. In fact, the book of 2 Chronicles can teach us to pray like kings and queens. 2 Chronicles showcases some excellent examples of prayer through various Kings like Solomon, Asa, Jehoshaphat and Queen Sheba.

Let's look first at King Solomon's prayer from 2 Chronicles 6. The context of Solomon's prayer is that he was born into a very challenging set of circumstances with an incredibly dysfunctional family. Yet, Solomon prayed for wisdom when God offered him anything he wanted. Solomon led all the people of Israel to worship God as he prayed. From Solomon's example, we see the importance of placing God on the throne of our heart – in terms of our posture of prayer, the opportunity for reflection of remembrance, to humble our heart, to intercede for others, the welcome for all and a chance for repentance of sin. God's reaction to Solomon's prayer is significant, as His glory filled the temple. God was delighted to see Solomon put God on the throne of his heart, which is the crucial decision we face daily. Next, we can learn from the example of the Queen of Sheba from 2 Chronicles 9. The Queen of Sheba had heard of Solomon's fame, so she came to see Solomon's wisdom for herself. She was shocked and overwhelmed by the ability that God had placed in Solomon. Her reaction to his excellence was to praise God, celebrate Him with upward praise, recognise the inward work God was doing within Solomon and behold how this outwardly blessed those around Solomon. Third, we can see how King Asa cried out to the God of heaven for help and how King Jehoshaphat prayed against all the odds. We can learn from their example that when we face trouble and trials, we look to the Lord for help in times of need. They took their challenges to God in prayer, keeping their eyes on God. Jehoshaphat showed that when we pray to remember, the battle is not ours but the Lord's. When we pray, we should be prepared personally by bearing with one another in the unity of the Spirit and walking in the light that He gives us to pray in faith and be obedient indeed. We, too, can learn from the lips of these kings and queens how to pray and seek the Lord.

An excellent example of how to pray like a king or queen is found in the account of King Hezekiah. We will look in-depth at how King Hezekiah prayed. We, too, can learn from Hezekiah's response in prayer as to how we can intercede and look to a Holy God in repentance. King Hezekiah's example of prayer is one of excellence. As we read these passages, please reflect on what stands out in your prayer life. What turn of phrase touches you? What parts of this grip you as we consider the urgency in the prayer of King Hezekiah from a place of risk to an Almighty God? How might this inspire your prayer life to cry out to God and ask for help in your times of need?

1. King Hezekiah's Committed Call

The context of this passage is that King Hezekiah is a good king of Judah. The Northern Kingdom of Israel was not following God's ways, but Hezekiah wanted all God's people to obey God. He called people from both kingdoms to celebrate Passover. A challenge to this plan was the lack of consecrated priests to complete the festival. So, here we join King Hezekiah's story in 2 Chronicles 30:6–9. We read, "At the king's command, couriers went throughout Israel and Judah with letters from the king and from his officials, which read: 'People of Israel, return to the Lord, the God of Abraham, Isaac and Israel, that He may return to you who are left, who have escaped from the hand of the kings of Assyria. Do not be like your parents and your fellow Israelites, who were unfaithful to the Lord, the God of their ancestors, so that he made them an object of horror, as you see. Do not be stiff-necked, as your ancestors were; submit to the Lord. Come to His sanctuary, which he has consecrated forever. Serve the Lord your God, so that His fierce anger will turn away from you. If you return to the Lord, then your fellow Israelites and your children will be shown compassion by their captors and will return to this land, for the Lord your God is gracious and compassionate. He will not turn His face from you if you return to Him."

King Hezekiah wants to include all of Israel and bring the people back to the Lord. He beseeches them not to reject God but to get right with Him directly. The solution to this is to submit to God. When was the last time you considered a situation and bowed the knee to the Father's will? Are we followers, or do we expect God to follow our plans? King Hezekiah called the people in verse eight to serve the Lord. When we pray, we pray with excellence when we have an orientation of submission to His will. King Hezekiah knew the Lord, and he knew His ways. Despite their previous rejection, God can welcome those who return to Him (v9). As we see from the Prodigal Son parable, Jesus shared that the heart of God is to welcome those who return to Him in repentance. God is a gracious God. Having the Father look graciously and with compassion in our lives is the best place to be. This can be dangerous and not often the easiest, but it is always the best. We can learn from King Hezekiah's example to trust in the compassionate character of God. Let's pray like King Hezekiah to call people to return to God.

2. King Hezekiah Believed Faithfully

Let's read on and consider the result of King Hezekiah's faithfulness in 2 Chronicles 30:10–20, "The couriers went from town to town in Ephraim and Manasseh, as far as Zebulun, but people scorned and ridiculed them. Nevertheless, some from Asher, Manasseh and Zebulun humbled themselves and went to Jerusalem. Also, in Judah, the hand of God was on the people to give them unity of mind to carry out what the king and his officials had ordered, following the word of the Lord. A huge crowd of people assembled in Jerusalem to celebrate the Festival of Unleavened Bread in the second month. They removed the altars in Jerusalem and cleared away the incense altars and threw them into the Kidron Valley. They slaughtered the Passover lamb on the fourteenth day of the second month. The priests and the Levites were ashamed and consecrated themselves and brought burnt offerings to the temple of the Lord. Then they took up their regular positions as prescribed in the Law of Moses, the man of God. The priests splashed against the altar the blood handed to them by the Levites. Since many in the crowd had not consecrated themselves, the Levites had to kill the Passover lambs for all those who were not ceremonially clean and could not consecrate their lambs to the Lord. Although most of the many people who came from Ephraim, Manasseh, Issachar, and Zebulun had not purified themselves, yet they ate the Passover, contrary to what was written. But Hezekiah prayed for them, saying, 'May the Lord, who is good, pardon everyone who sets their heart on seeking God – the Lord, the God of their ancestors – even if they are not clean according to the rules of the sanctuary.' And the Lord heard Hezekiah and healed the people."

King Hezekiah's desire for all the people to return to God is met with scorn. His simple and faithful requests for the people to celebrate Passover are rejected in each place it is offered. We must be prepared for refusal when we pray and act in faith. However, just like in the parable of the Sower, some seed falls on the healthy soil of the heart. There are those in Asher, Manasseh and Zebulun who humbly chose to follow God's law and celebrate Passover. When we step forward in faith, God will show us where He is working. We will have testimonies of His provision and fruitfulness.

Furthermore, we see that God blesses the faithfulness of King Hezekiah with a spiritually galvanising impact of unity on the people of Judah. In taking steps of faith, God blesses those around us when we step forward. The people are stirred to follow God's word, gather together, reject idol sacrifice and worship the Lord in the Passover festival. God honours Hezekiah's faith to impact leaders and followers, as the Priests are drawn to consecrate themselves ready for the celebration. Prayer leads people to excellence before the Lord. However, many people were not ceremonially clean before the Lord for the Passover. There had been years of unfaithfulness across Israel; Hezekiah's father, King Ahaz of Judah, had led the people to worship idols as had every king before and following in the Northern Kingdom of Israel.

Solomon came in and consecrated the temple, the priests, and the people. He prays at the end of verse eighteen for the purification of the people before a Holy God. Hezekiah's prayer recognises the people's sin and the state of the nation. Hezekiah prays, "May the Lord pardon everyone." His prayer acknowledges the holiness of God and, in faith, a need for forgiveness. When we pray, we need to humble ourselves in prayer. It is instructive to pray like a faithful king who humbly asks God if He would pardon the people. King Hezekiah knows that an act of mercy is needed rather than an order for the people to be pardoned. When we pray, let's humbly ask an all-powerful God to act. King Hezekiah trusts that God can read the hearts of those he is praying for. He gives over this decision-making to God, which pleases God. The people needed healing from their sin and God answered King Hezekiah's prayer. When we pray, let's pray with a faithful heart and in humility to an Almighty God.

3. King Jesus Prayed Earnestly

We can learn so much from King Jesus' example in prayer also. Jesus taught the disciples how to pray as we can see with the Lord's prayer. But Jesus practised what He preached and would spend a lot of time in prayer with the

Father. Jesus knew the battle was as much on His knees in prayer as it was in debate with the Pharisees or the Devil in the wilderness. On the very night He washed the disciple's feet and just hours before He was betrayed and handed over to the Romans by Judas, Jesus prayed. He prayed in three sections: for Himself, His disciples and then all believers.

John 17:1–5

"After Jesus said this, He looked toward heaven and prayed: 'Father, the hour has come. Glorify Your Son, that Your Son may glorify You. For You granted Him authority over all people that He might give eternal life to all those You have given Him. Now this is eternal life: that they know You, the only true God, and Jesus Christ, whom You have sent. I have brought You glory on earth by finishing the work You gave Me to do. And now, Father, glorify Me in Your presence with the glory I had with You before the world began.'"

Here, Jesus positions Himself toward God in Heaven. Jesus' posture is one of sincerity of faith and intimacy with His Father. He knows He exists and He calls out to Him by name. Jesus calls forward the specific mission God has given Him to do as He prays "The hour has come." Jesus prays through what the mission was (v2–3) and how it has gone (v4). When we pray, it is not like God does not already know the content of what we pray but in fact as we process what has happened and is happening, He can bring revelation of what is next to happen. Furthermore, reflecting on what has been achieved often reminds us of God's favour in our journey, and this can lead to spontaneous opportunities for praise and thankfulness for the ways God has intervened with provision. Jesus progresses on to pray for those closest to Him.

John 17:6–10

"I have revealed You to those whom You gave Me out of the world. They were Yours; You gave them to Me, and they have obeyed Your word. Now they know that everything You have given Me comes from You. For I gave them the words You gave Me and they accepted them. They knew with certainty that I came from You, and they believed that You sent Me. I pray for them. I am not praying for the world but for those You have given Me, for they are Yours. All I have is Yours, and all You have is Mine. And glory has come to Me through them."

Jesus recognises that God has put these disciples in His life to work with. He prays for them and serves them. Jesus' example of obedience ministers to His disciples, but it is the spiritual change in their hearts that God enables that breathes life into their souls. The disciples can now see that Jesus is the Messiah, and Jesus commends them to God. In fact, those who are Jesus' disciples not only bring glory to God the Father but also to Jesus the Son. Jesus prayed for His disciples then, and He prays for His disciples now. Christians are disciples of Christ, and we can follow His example, grow in our understanding of who He is through the Bible and have access to the Holy Spirit, who reminds us of Jesus' teaching. Jesus does not stop there, though; He prays for those yet to believe.

John 17:20–21

"My prayer is not for them alone. I pray also for those who will believe in Me through their message, that all of them may be one, Father, just as You are in Me and I am in You. May they also be in Us so that the world may believe that You have sent Me."

Jesus desires that all may come to Him. He does not just pray for His disciples; He prays for future believers who are impacted by the message of the Good News. Jesus wants all people to experience the transformational joy of knowing the Father and being one with the Son. Jesus has revealed God's master plan and provides the opportunity for us to be reconciled to God at the Cross. Within days of praying these prayers, Jesus was executed at the cross but triumphantly rose to life to usher in a new reality of hope and freedom for all who believe. Jesus' prayer was urgent, it was a petition for salvation. Whatever experience, good or ill, we have had of our earthly father, we, too, like Jesus, can rest in the Heavenly Father, who is trustworthy and available to hear, see, and deliver us, those closest to us and others across the world. Jesus had just days to live, but He prioritised prayer over action. It is worth prioritising God in whichever situations we will face this week. Let's consider what this week looks like and pray through those in our lives. Don't delay; pray like a king this week.

Summary

In closing, let's remember to pray like the kings and queens who were faithful to God. Let's place God on the throne of our hearts like King Solomon; let's pray upward, inward, and outward like the Queen of Sheba; let's cry out in prayer even against all the odds like King Asa and King Jehoshaphat; and finally, as we've looked at in-depth, let's call others and believe faithfully like King Hezekiah, and pray earnestly like King Jesus. Remember, if you are a follower of Jesus, you are a prince or princess in the Kingdom of Heaven. Prayer is the secret to excellence. Let's not just have this as head knowledge but apply it in our hearts to draw close to God and serve others.

PART FIVE
| INTENTION |

JOE LOWTHER

Chapter 9
Intention: KICK's Story

Intentional relationships are a vital value for KICK because young people aged sixteen to twenty-four are more likely than any other age group to feel lonely often/always. We must be intentional in our interactions for the sake of young people. Loneliness increases[22] stress levels, social withdrawal, decreased self-esteem, disrupts healthy eating, negatively impacts physical health and raises the risk of suicide.[23] We must not fail to be intentional with young people. We have a responsibility in how we work towards bringing our community closer together by being intentional in all our relationships. In the Old Testament, God outlines that He wants to form communities together to be more fruitful (Genesis 28:3). The ten commandments outline how God wants us to live in order to have effective relationships. In the New Testament Jesus has intentional relationships with His disciples as He trains them. He specifically teaches His followers and heals every aliment of those brought to Him. Jesus brings communities together to form one body, His church, where every member belongs and has a part to play (Romans 12:5). There is rich variety and diversity in His body but all people are equally loved, even if their knowledge and experience of His blessings may vary. All are welcome in His community if we choose to follow Him (1 Corinthians 12:12–26). Jesus establishes a way of relating where His followers operate as a family – mourning in tragedy and rejoicing in success together (Romans 12:15–16). The depth of experience of this in any group will depend in part on each individual's willingness to participate and respond to God's love and direction. At KICK this is our model. It is to be thought through by individual staff and also us as a team to move to deepening commitment to be intentional in our interactions with young people. We believe God uses intentional relationships as we work together, with partners and with young people. Our mission seeks to see young people integrate across all generations (2 Chronicles 31:18), as we are convinced this is for their benefit. We must be intentional to engage young people effectively.

1. Learn Romanian? No Problem!

In Slough Secondary School, there were many Romanian Romany refugees. One of our coaches, Lillie, was brought in to mentor the young people. As she engaged, sometimes discussions were tough to cover in broken English. At other times, the boys would say things in Romanian that would clearly cut at the heart of the girls. Not being able to understand these phrases or get to the root of the problems, Lillie enrolled in a Romanian language course on her own initiative. Her focus was to relate to the young people better. Lillie inspired us all with her dedication and focus to be intentional in her relationships. They opened up to her as she engaged with the young people in their own language. She had made the effort; they felt cared for and more able to share what was going on. Practical, intentional compassion is so crucial to building trust.

Furthermore, she was able to respond to the taunts thrown at some of the young girls, and the boys felt shocked that they had been outed in what they were saying. They had a new respect for Lillie and responded to her rebuke. This led to powerful follow-up conversations about respect for women and was an opportunity to challenge stereotypes. By showing such dedicated commitment, these boys felt valued, and this fresh dignity brought a constructive change in the more respectful way they spoke to the girls.

2. Planting a Mustard Seed

In a story of intention, Trustee Penny Cox said, "Back in 2004, I remember our Vicar, the amazing faith-filled Rev. Trevor Patterson, standing before the congregation at Holy Trinity Richmond, sharing the idea of starting a KICK Academy at church. Trevor was passionate about young people knowing Jesus and he was grieved by the fact that children and teenagers were going to sports clubs instead of attending church. So here was the vision: our church would work together with KICK so that young people could do both and even go one step better – have a Christian coach who could guide and mentor them in their spiritual walk while enhancing their footballing skills. Trevor was so convinced that this was God's work that he even changed the start time of our morning service by half an hour to facilitate the KICK Academy! Seeing the children and young people's relationship with the church, the coach and Christ grow through this initiative was wonderful. I can still hear the clatter of football boots on the floor as the children left the church at the end of the services. As news of the KICK Academy spread, other young people from outside the church community began to attend, so they also heard about

Jesus. Here we are twenty years later, and KICK now has the opportunity to engage more than twenty-eight thousand five hundred young people per week. God has mightily blessed this mustard seed of faith and reminded us that nothing is impossible with Him."

3. I Don't Like Cricket; I Hate It

Let me tell you about Lucas. Lucas was a bright kid, but his parents divorced and he became angry. Angry with his father and his situation. Lucas began to get involved in risky behaviours and started taking drugs. Lucas' habit grew, and he was forced to pay for that habit by dealing drugs himself. As a result, he was referred to mentoring. His mentor built trust and spoke truth into his life, challenging his choices from a place of kindness. According to the Government's Lessons From London Report[24] 3–6pm is the most dangerous time of the week for children and young people. Lucas dealt drugs during this window. His mentor challenged this and encouraged Lucas to come to his after-school club in cricket. He'd say, "Come on, Lucas, come play cricket," each week. Lucas responded, "No, I don't like cricket." The mentor persisted to the point where Lucas blurted out, "OK, I'll come, but not for cricket, but because of you." Lucas was a natural, so much so that he now opens the batting and the bowling for his school. Lucas was now too busy to deal drugs, practising twice a week and focusing on his fitness. This is a story of how intentional relationships can have a transforming impact on young people's lives.

4. Baptism of Fire

A school in crisis measures asked for KICK to provide a chaplain. The school's headteacher had suffered life-changing injuries, and a new headteacher needed support with the pastoral issues generated. Samuel joined the school as chaplain and became a beacon of hope and gentle support for pupils, parents and teachers. The new headteacher, a non-Christian, was so struck by Samuel's evident faith in Jesus that he asked to meet with Samuel to do a weekly Bible study. Being intentional is necessary to make the most of every opportunity; we were proud of Samuel's example.

Our chaplains follow the seven nationally recognised dimensions of school-based chaplaincy, which are pastoral, worshipful, spiritual, missional, servant-hearted, prophetic and educational. This often means that they play a crucial role in prophetically standing up for the ethos of their schools in decision-making. One of our chaplains, based across two schools, could share the Gospel with one thousand five hundred young people in one week at Easter. What church leader can share the Gospel with one thousand five hundred people per week? Samuel recalled that in another school, "A young person came to speak with me as a chaplain with her friend. She told me that she was raped in Year Nine. We set up a team around the child and worked closely with her parents. As a chaplain, I continued to provide support through prayer, the love of Jesus, and a listening ear. She started going to a local church, and she ended up getting baptised. She asked for the Vicar and I, as chaplain, to baptise her. I was amazed to see young people have a real relationship with Jesus." Being a chaplain is a phenomenal chance to transform young people's lives. Alex Shoderu, another KICK chaplain, can provide Chaplaincy provision in the mornings, mentors some of the most challenging pupils in the afternoon and then delivers rugby after school clubs. His headteacher has said that the chaplain has gone from being one of the last people the learners confide into, to being the first. Providing strong role models who love Jesus is an excellent opportunity to intentionally transform lives.

5. Rugby: A Version of Self-Harm

KICK mentor Peter Brooks had one of the most revered learners in his school referred to him for mentoring – the First XV Rugby Team Captain. This young person was famous throughout the school for his bravery. He would throw himself into rucks with abandon for his teammates. He had experienced three concussions and various stud marks from being raked at mauls. Why was this school hero referred to for mentoring? Pete met with him and built trust, which led to him eventually opening up that rugby was his version of self-harm. He smashed into those rucks to punish himself. His best friend had died in a car accident, and the boy didn't understand why he was alive and his friend wasn't.

Tormented by the pain of his friend's death, he used rugby as a means to take away his mental pain through physical agony. Pete was able to gently question whether his best friend would have wanted him to be in pain. No one knew what this learner was going through. No one had had the chance to ask that question. Now, the learner could think this through and consider this reality. These opportunities present the chance to be intentional in our relationships. Another young person whom Pete worked with suffered with anxiety through affluent neglect from his parents. Pete read Psalm 46 to him and prayed for healing in his life. He felt drawn to give him a Bible but didn't want to overstep his position as chaplain. The boy prayed, and that very weekend, the young person met a Nigerian street evangelist who gave him a Bible. Following that, it was clear how the boy's faith evolved, and the peace God had given him as he grew. Every interaction we have is a chance to make a transformational impact.

6. Broken Glass

Hope Church, Hounslow, launched a KICK Academy and faithfully provided sports ministry to seven young people per week. Frustrated by a housing development on the nice park they played in, they had been shunted across to a green where they needed to move dog faeces and clear broken glass that teenagers had smashed the night before. Then, lockdown kicked in, and every community-based sports provision was forced to close. Post lockdown, they decided it might be easiest to stay closed. Was it necessary now, with so many other priorities, to focus on post-COVID-19? There was an outcry from parents. They begged them to reopen. The children had been locked up for the best part of a year and were desperate to be physically fit and active once more. As the KICK Academy reopened, they realised it was not just these parents but many others in their community who were desperate for their young people to express energy. In week one, thirteen kids came; in week two, twenty-two;

in week three, twenty-eight kids. The KICK Academy had to limit it to eighty-five children a week. They now have primary and secondary age teams and saw some of those children got baptised this past year. Their volunteers are delighted to shift dog faeces and have a spring in their step as they clear broken glass. Their mission is impacting their community.

7. Coachee to Coach

KICK coach Jack Newman is a fine example of progression from young person to coach at KICK. His story is one of integrity, and he can talk straight into the lives of our young people. He said, "When I was seven years old, my Auntie Sarah attended the local church Merland Rise and invited me to a new KICK Academy for my first experience of football and faith. The KICK Academy enhanced my faith in Jesus. Hearing about faith every week in a day-to-day sense made faith normal to me. Sport and faith became tangible and linked together. It taught me to pick my friends wisely and distance myself from unhelpful influences. At fourteen years old, I transitioned from being a player to a volunteer coach. At sixteen, the church paid for my FA Level One badges to become a qualified coach. I was then inspired to become a professional coach at KICK after realising I could focus through the week on my passion – coaching. I joined KICK in 2021 when I was eighteen years old and have found this foundational in terms of my career and my faith. I feel that I have purpose and that KICK has transformed my life over these fourteen years."

8. Heads and Tales

Young people are struggling with anxiety for a variety of reasons. Mentor Becks Louis underlines, "I was mentoring a girl who had recently been in a dangerous accident where she was slammed into a pillar and cracked her head. I prayed for peace. She went into hospital and spent six weeks in recovery. When she returned, she had to come and rest. She wouldn't say that she got scared easily, but she was very fearful of this being a life-changing injury. I prayed for peace and healing, and it was moving to see her return to school and be freed from the long-term effects she experienced. Prayers are powerful. Fully believing in faith and trusting in a God who cares, makes a difference." Young people grow up in an environment of suspicion and mistrust of authority. It requires a commitment to be intentional in our relationships, and Mentor Louise Corless is a great example. Louise recalled, "I mentored an eleven-year-old girl who was struggling to maintain friendships and show care to others. I soon learnt it was all about building trust and showing her compassion as, sadly, she didn't experience this at home. I focused our sessions on relationships, emotions and the future she desires. I made sure to listen to her aspirations and dreams. I encouraged her to do the same with others by showing her compassion. Slowly, she began to maintain friendships, be kind to others and think positively about the future. The school was so happy with her progress that she has now completed her mentoring provision."

9. Losing Rags to Empathic Riches

Coach Joe Mallett reflects on the context of intention, stating that when interacting with young people, we must challenge with intention based on empathy. He explains, "I've been mentoring one young person for two years now, and before I started with him, he would lose his rag extremely quickly at the slightest of things not going his way. He could disrupt a lesson and make everyone around him unhappy because he didn't get his way. He couldn't control his anger; he couldn't understand it, making him more frustrated. I made it my goal to be intentional with him, not only in mentoring but in spending time with him in PE lessons, clubs and lunchtime; we'd talk, we'd watch videos, we'd get other kids involved and speak about how it made them feel and how it looked to them. This intentionality really paid off. He began to trust me and implement some of the strategies we'd discussed. I think it helped him develop self-awareness, an understanding of what's going on and how to better manage his feelings and emotions. He's come on leaps and bounds. He is very empathetic towards others now and eager to congratulate and shake hands with opponents, win or lose."

Summary

These stories inspire us to be intentional in the relationships we are privileged to have. Every interaction is critical to the well-being of struggling young people who need time and attention. We are motivated to do so because of the understanding of God's love for us and the innate value that He created life. To be intentional is to imitate God and treat people with dignity and respect.

JOE LOWTHER

Chapter 10
Intention: Spiritual Application

Being intentional in our relationships is a principle of how God works with us and how He instructs us to work with each other. We see this clearly in Nehemiah and the examples of Nicodemus and Simon of Cyrene at the Cross. Starting with Nehemiah 3, the context of these events is that God gave Nehemiah a vision to rebuild the walls of Jerusalem. God intentionally cares about the safety of His people. As we read this, don't be sidetracked with the range of long names. Instead, listen to the passage as you read, and hang in there. Think about the builders' different personalities and diverse occupations, and how many were stone masons?

Let's read Nehemiah 3:1–12, "Eliashib the high priest and his fellow priests went to work and rebuilt the Sheep Gate. They dedicated it and set its doors in place, building as far as the Tower of the Hundred, which they dedicated, and as far as the Tower of Hananel. The men of Jericho built the adjoining section, and Zakkur son of Imri built next to them. The Fish Gate was rebuilt by the sons of Hassenaah. They laid its beams and put its doors and bolts and bars in place. Meremoth son of Uriah, the son of Hakkoz, repaired the next section. Next to him Meshullam son of Berekiah, the son of Meshezabel, made repairs, and next to him Zadok son of Baana also made repairs. The next section was repaired by the men of Tekoa, but their nobles would not put their shoulders to the work under their supervisors. The Jeshanah Gate was repaired by Joiada son of Paseah and Meshullam son of

Besodeiah. They laid its beams and put its doors with their bolts and bars in place. Next to them, repairs were made by men from Gibeon and Mizpah – Melatiah of Gibeon and Jadon of Meronoth – places under the authority of the governor of Trans-Euphrates. Uzziel son of Harhaiah, one of the goldsmiths, repaired the next section; and Hananiah, one of the perfume-makers, made repairs next to that. They restored Jerusalem as far as the Broad Wall. Rephaiah son of Hur, ruler of a half-district of Jerusalem, repaired the next section. Adjoining this, Jedaiah son of Harumaph made repairs opposite his house, and Hattush son of Hashabneiah made repairs next to him. Malkijah son of Harim and Hasshub son of Pahath-Moab repaired another section and the Tower of the Ovens. Shallum son of Hallohesh, ruler of a half-district of Jerusalem, repaired the next section with the help of his daughters."

In reading this passage, we can be struck by how intentionally personal it is. God spends a whole chapter on this level of detail and names specific people throughout. Nehemiah 3 can speak to us through three personal factors: intentional service, choice and calling.

1. Intentional Service

The first of these factors is intentional service. In verse one to four, Nehemiah organised the people into teams for different sections of the wall. Nehemiah writes "next to him", "next to him", "next to them" – they were in close proximity to each other. They served intentionally and in proximity. Building the wall involved a wide range of people who all laid down their professions for the communal safety of the city and in obedience to God's plans. They served each other, built together, regardless of their starting point or profession – they all contributed. Priests, goldsmiths, perfume-makers, district rulers, guards and merchants were all dedicated to the task. We can see this in the body of Christ, too. The church of Christ is more of an organism than an organisation. It is designed to be a full-body dynamic, with all included to play their part in the calling God has set out. As we stand in proximity, let's serve one another and be prepared to do something we are not skilled at, to honour the body of God's people.

God wants us to know Him directly, personally. He is jealous for our attention and desires relationship with us. Like any genuinely loving father, God enjoys time with His children. He warns us to avoid distractions or, worse, things that would lead us away from Him and damage us. In 1 Corinthians 2:16, Paul talks about the importance and the joy of knowing the mind of Christ. As our Father, God wants us to know His approaches and understand His ways so that we can be close to Him and grow up in a strong and secure way in His love. Jesus pleased God so much because, as His Son, He knew His Father's mind. If we know the Mind of Christ, we can listen to the Father's instruction and follow His ways. This is a series of decisions to honour God, to know God more profoundly or remain at the shallow end of our relationship with Him. The tide pushes us back from knowing God and following His ways, so we need to keep reminding ourselves to follow Him.

A helpful case study from the Gospels is that of Nicodemus. He was a pharisee who broke the mould to seek after Jesus. He took the dangerous step to intentionally go at night to meet Jesus, to know Him and His ways. In John 3:2, he said, "Rabbi, we know that You are a teacher who has come from God" and he quizzed Jesus on how people could enter the Kingdom of Heaven. Nicodemus wanted to know God, and this is when Jesus said to him that we must be spiritually reborn to enter God's Kingdom as reported in John 3. John later summarised in verse sixteen Jesus' mission, "God so loved the world that He gave His only Son, that whoever believes in Him should not perish but have eternal life." Then we hear about Nicodemus twice more in the New Testament – once in John 7:50 when Nicodemus is faced with a choice to make his faith public – do I follow Jesus or quit. He takes a stand and defends Jesus, reprimanding the other Pharisees for trying to insight a mob to kill Jesus; secondly, in John 19 – where it was actually Nicodemus who carried out the burial of Christ using the myrrh, which prophetically had been given by the wise men at Jesus' birth. Nicodemus wanted to know Jesus and demonstrated this in his faith to stand up for Him in front of his hostile colleagues, and again, even after Jesus had died at His Tomb. When following Jesus is challenging, will we stand to say that we know Him? When Jesus does not appear close in your life, will you believe He loves you? God is the Author of creation. He is intentional in His relationships with us. He wants us to know Him and demonstrate this through faith.

2. Intentional choice

The second factor is intentional choice. Back in Nehemiah 3:5, we know some of the nobles who resisted the opportunity to serve. What effect does this have when we resist what God asks of us and don't step up? How can we resolve ourselves to do what God wants us to do? An example to illustrate this is King Solomon. He was given all wisdom, and there has been none like him about wisdom; however, after a good start, he resisted following God's ways, which led to disaster for the people he led. Being wise is irrelevant if we don't choose to obey God. Proverbs 9:10 underlines this as it states, "The fear of the Lord is the beginning of wisdom" and Proverbs 1:7 says, "Fools despise wisdom and instruction." Following God is the outworking of wisdom; to reject Him, the Bible describes this as foolish. May Solomon be a warning to us.

Furthermore, we don't have to be intelligent or powerful to be faithful to God. He takes us where we are and gives wisdom to those who ask Him for it. James 1:5 says, "If any of you lacks wisdom, you should ask God, who gives generously to all without finding fault and it will be given to you." From this place of choice, God gives freely to all and without fault. What an offer we have available. Will we choose to ask?

God wants to provide all that we need. Leviticus 26:3–6 says, "If you follow My decrees and are careful to obey My commands, I will send you rain in its season, and the ground will yield its crops and the trees their fruit. Your threshing will continue until grape harvest and the grape harvest will continue until planting, and you will eat all the food you want and live in safety in your land. I will grant peace in the land, and you will lie down, and no one will make you afraid." God also wants to protect us from harm wherever we are. This is the same Father God that desires a relationship with you today. The key question is, will you choose Him? As we can see from Jesus' life, walking as a Christian is not devoid of suffering; this is often a part of living a faithful life to God in a world which is so often hostile to Him. God wants to bless us. It is His promise, as we have seen in verse three, that if we "follow God's decrees and are careful to obey His commands", we will be blessed by Him. It is important for us to grasp that God's blessings are both general – to all His created children – and also specific. There are conditions sometimes to receiving some blessings as this passage illustrates (v3–4), "If you... I will..." God's love is unconditional, He loves all people and creatures that He has made. At creation He took great pleasure as He saw that they were good. However, He also desires to draw humankind back to Himself, to restore some of the blessings that result from the right relationship with God, including for those who have committed their lives to Him and have decided to walk in His ways and directions. He is sensitive to the individuality of all people and to the reason for their unique experiences and circumstances. He desires to be responsive and caring in each life and in various situations but will not force Himself on anyone who is not interested. The Bible says that God knocks on the door of our hearts. He is eager to come in and bless our lives, providing what we need in times of trouble. He does not always provide the jam or butter, but He always provides the bread we need when we are walking in His ways.

Another story of someone you might not have thought much about before is that of Mary Magdalene. Mary Magdalene was a sex-worker, which led to shame and mockery in her culture. She was possessed by seven demons until Jesus set her free. From then on, she was a committed follower of Jesus right through to being present at His death on the cross when many had deserted Him. Mary mourned Jesus and went to the tomb early to visit His body, but she was the first to see that the stone had been rolled away from the tomb. She runs to tell the disciples and is shocked by what she must only imagine is some further cruel torture by the Romans. However, it is none other than Mary Magdalene who is the first person to whom Jesus reveals Himself. While grieving at the empty tomb, she finds the two angels present and then, without realising, talks with Jesus. The way He reveals Himself to her is so tender and personal. He simply says "Mary" and she instantly knows the sound of His voice. Jesus then instructs her to go and tell the disciples that He has risen and will soon ascend to Heaven. Jesus calls her by name and has plans for her to be a part of His big story. Mary was very different to Nicodemus. I love that here are two very different but committed friends of Jesus who were there at Jesus' execution, from very different backgrounds, who both had a part to play and followed God. A woman from an impoverished background full of shame and a pious scholar, a man from a privileged circumstance. Jesus desired that both come to Him.

Regardless of where we are from, are we prepared to be present with Jesus? Are we there, ready to run to Him and point others to do the same? Are we available to be intentional with Jesus as He is with us? If Mary Magdalene had not come to the tomb, she would have missed out on this unique opportunity to see the resurrected Messiah Jesus – the first to do so in fact. Mary followed and was a part of God's master plan to revolutionise history and bring us back to Him. As the people at the wall with Nehemiah made their choices, Mary Magdalene made her choice and followed Jesus – will you?

3. Intentional Calling

The third factor is intentional calling. We are intentionally called by God for specific tasks. In Nehemiah 3:6–8, we see these people were from different backgrounds. Still, they were all aligned with a single purpose: the glory of God. This is a brilliant picture of how God's people should be. The Israelites finished the wall in fifty-two days whilst holding swords and using shovels. They were armed for battle at any moment but working together. Let's remember to be ready for whatever battles arise as we build together as one. How are we preparing for battle? In verse twelve, Shallum completed his section with his daughters. There was urgency and dedication to the job; it was all hands to the pump. What is the part of the wall God is asking you to build in His Kingdom? How are we at KICK to work well beside one another? How can you change to accommodate others in the tasks we are called to do? God may well call you and equip you for tasks outside of your comfort zone. Sometimes, God may call us in line with our gifting, and sometimes not. Nehemiah was trained as a sommelier, and suddenly, here he was called to manage a construction project, very much outside of his experience and skills. It is often in such circumstances that we are more in need of trust in God for provision ahead of our natural abilities and, as a result, are able to recognise His work in our lives.

We can read in Leviticus 26:11–13 that God said, "I will put My dwelling place among you, and I will not abhor you. I will walk among you and be your God, and you will be My people. I am the Lord your God, who brought you out of Egypt so that you would no longer be slaves to the Egyptians; I broke the bars of your yoke and enabled you to walk with heads held high." As we intentionally follow God, this is where He lives with us. This is such a mind-blowing reality to have a personal calling from Him where He dwells with us. When the Israelites were in the Wilderness, God would physically dwell in their presence in the big Tabernacle tent. The Israelite tribes encamped around the Tabernacle as the central tent. There was a cloud by day and fire by night to intentionally remind the people where God was. When it moved, they moved with it. God wants to dwell and walk with us. He wants us to be His people, and we all have the opportunity to do this now through His Holy Spirit. We can be encouraged today by the example He gives in verse thirteen – of how He led the Israelites out of slavery and set them free. This wonderful picture of the bars of the yoke, which trapped them, held them down and imprisoned them, were broken by His hand. So that they were not just free but could hold their heads up high. What holds you down today? What traps you? Is it a broken relationship? Some unforgiveness? A pornography addiction? God wants to break these bars that enslave you and enable you to hold your head up high.

Summary

God cares about you and desires to dwell with us all intentionally. So, let's know Him like Nicodemus, follow Him like Mary Magdalene and see Him dwell with us more deeply today. Let's be inspired by the example of Nehemiah 3:20; we have a summary of Baruch, son of Zabbai, who is praised as doing his work zealously to repair another section for the entrance of the house of Eliashib, the high priest. Wouldn't we all like to be referred to in these glowing terms? We are asked to build God's Kingdom today, and wouldn't it be an honour to be described as zealous in this task? God has intentionally prepared personal acts of service in advance for us to do. When deciding whether or not to follow Him, we have an individual choice to make. Let's embrace our personal calling to intentionally build His Kingdom zealously.

PART SIX
| INTEGRITY |

JOE LOWTHER

Chapter 11
Integrity: KICK's Story

We must be intentional towards young people's personal and social needs. Generation Z face an era of seismic change and opportunity but struggle to find places of safety and courage to be resilient. With so much change and so much uncertainty, they need authenticity and integrity. Therefore, we must make decisions with character and integrity to be heard and begin a journey towards real spiritual change. Young people face personal and social challenges, but they also face spiritual problems. 46.2% of Brits identified themselves as Christians, down from 59.3%, a thirteen percent decade drop.[25] However, only six percent would be considered practising Christians. Only 4.5% of young people go to Church in the UK[26] and at the same time, there is growing anxiety among young people about what life is all about. God has such Good News to share and wants to give so many answers to the climate crisis, mental health and social justice. But the poor cultural positioning and or flatlining opportunities for church engagement in the UK are contributing to children leaving church. Children and young people are now seven times more likely to play sport at the weekend, rather than engage in Church. Church attendance is down in the UK and an example of this is most starkly recognised with news that only four hundred and thirty confirmations in the Church of Scotland took place in 2021 compared with forty thousand at the peak in the 1930s, with an average age attendance of sixty-two.[27] Therefore, we must have integrity in our provision to make a transformational difference in the lives of young people.

Jesus Christ had great integrity (Matt 22:16) and spoke boldly in what He believed in (Matt 10:34,39). He was consistently faithful to His Father and those around Him (Rev 1:5). Jesus' honesty shone through. He repeatedly resisted opportunities to speak ill of someone behind their back as He said, "I have spoken openly...I said nothing in secret" (John 18:20). Jesus Himself was stirred by matters of justice and stood up for the oppressed and against the oppressor, challenging the authorities and societal constructs of His day (John 2:13–17). Jesus condemned hypocrisy and abuse of power targeting the Pharisees, calling out their duplicity and hardness of heart. God appointed people due to their integrity (Nehemiah 7:2). Paul speaks of people with integrity as good role models (Titus 2:6–8); thus, we take integrity seriously as a defining value.

1. Treble the Need

Compelled out of integrity to make a difference, Trustee Cliff Underhay was drawn to commit twenty years of his life. Cliff remembers, "A Men's Breakfast in 2005 was held at West Wickham and Shirley Baptist Church, led by founding coach Tom Rutter. Then tragedy struck – fifteen-year-old Gavin Banton Brown was stabbed to death in a Croydon playground in front of fifty children. This crystalised a response from the five churches within a mile of the incident. A management team was established to raise funds to employ Croydon's first Development Officer in 2006. Interviews were held whilst, at the same time, an application was made to a Croydon-based grant funder for one year's funding. As the interview date neared and we had not secured funding, we wondered what to do. We duly went ahead with the interview planning, and God truly confirmed our plans by granting us funding from CRIN. However, we got the £25,000 we applied for and were informed that the funder would support us for three years and granted us £75,000! Hans Sims (New Life Christian Centre) was duly appointed." There are many more stories of God's glorious provision. God has been faithful, and we must remain faithful to Him. We should not just stand by and allow young people to struggle. If we are called by Him, our acts of faith are a response in stepping forward in integrity to God's plans.

2. Every Child Has the Right to Learn

Every person has innate value because they are created and loved by God. At KICK in all our interactions we must be faithful to this reality. Coach Alastair Park illustrates an opportunity to show this: "When my first-choice goalkeeper was ill on the day of a tournament, it was a hard choice to select who would take his place. There was one boy who hadn't been selected before, and he also had autism. He loved football and always played in goal at lunchtime. So, I decided to take him. I wasn't expecting to win, but I expected all the children to include him as one of the team members, which they did. The group stages went well, and we won all of our games, getting us through the knockout stages. The final was tough, and it was 0–0, meaning it was a penalty shootout. I spoke to the boy and said he didn't need to if the pressure was too much, but he wanted to do it for his team. He saved all three penalties, and we won the tournament. All the boys sprinted over to this boy and hugged and chanted his name. The boy was smiling from ear to ear, making his year. He left year six and said that that was his favourite memory."

3. Parliament APPG

As KICK grew nationally, we were invited by the wonderfully talented and sadly late Lea Milligan, to be a part of the All-Party Parliamentary Group (APPG) for the impact of COVID-19 on young people's mental and physical well-being. KICK was the only Christian organisation on the APPG and had a unique opportunity to speak about harrowing situations. We looked at painful topics such as the rise in teen suicide, sexual abuse against girls and the high incarceration in prison of boys. We have been invited three times to contribute to chapters on government papers for future policy reviews, making recommendations on how to respond to adolescent childhood experiences. We have commented on the importance of sport and dance in processing one's mental health through physical health, the impact of mental health through mentoring, and the emphasis on the value of chaplaincy as a spiritual response to the lockdowns. Recently, we were invited to speak at Westminster about the importance of girls in sports. As I walked through the Houses of Parliament, I was struck that between the House of Commons and the House of Lords, there is a marble square which has Psalm 127:1 embossed on the floor. It reads, "Unless the Lord builds the house, the builder labour in vain. Unless the Lord watches over the city, the guards stand watch in vain." It was a reminder that when Oliver Cromwell founded his new form of Parliamentary Government in 1653, God was to be at the centre of decision-making in the United Kingdom. I understand that he created the role of Government Minister because the term means to minister to people in service on behalf of God. We must continue to pray for opportunity for today's MPs to remember this remit and I was encouraged that this Psalm is a reminder for two Houses of power at Westminster.

4. Coaching Growth

From a position of integrity, to impact young people, we must develop staff with KICK's values at their heart. Mark Anderson, KICK's Operations Manager from 2010–2014, outlines a good example: "KICK is all about transforming young people's lives, with God's love, through sport and support. However, it also means KICK's impact on the young coaches and mentors who deliver the sessions in those places. In about 2010, a coach joined KICK on a placement. He was born overseas, was in his late teens, and had settled in London, where he joined KICK on a short-term placement. Under the guidance of experienced staff coaches, he helped to lead parts of sessions, growing in confidence and ability. The Christian witness of KICK coaches also had an impact on him. The time this young coach spent with KICK staff, the prayers, the opportunities given to him, and the belief put in him all contributed to God doing wonderful things in the life of this young person whose future could have been so different had he not been transformed by God's love through KICK." Another coach, Denzil Dooley, brought the love of God into every interaction he engaged with.

Schools would remember the impact of Denzil years later. He developed so much during his time with KICK, but it was clear that God was at work in his life. Denzil was drawn to head back to South Africa. Since returning home, he has started a sports ministry called Aslan, which works with deprived young people in townships. We were delighted to work together again in 2023 to launch our first international 4 KICK Academies in South Africa.

5. North East Engagement

We are delighted to see our work grow in the North East, especially as two of our key founding pioneers of KICK in London twenty years ago originated there in Jon Burns and Barry Mason. Now, coach Adam Charlton shares his thoughts on the importance of challenging behaviours with integrity: "This has been a key part of helping children to be physically active and enjoy their PE lessons, as when we first returned to school post lockdown, there was a lot of low-level disruptive behaviour and a lot more disengagement/uncertainty of how to participate in a group setting again. A great example of this was a year five child who, during lockdown, struggled to engage with remote learning and rarely left home/participated in any physical activity. When returning to school, he was very anxious, and engagement in lessons was very low. He would quite often not have a PE kit and refused to participate. However, after implementing more soft skills and character development through mentoring and focusing more on this in lessons, I have seen its impact. He now always has a PE kit and shows enthusiasm and enjoyment in his PE lessons. His engagement has grown in other lessons, and he has become more confident in himself and how to interact with others. There are still moments when he struggles with anxiety, but he has made great progress. It has been great to see children of all abilities and levels engaged in PE lessons, both from a physical perspective and a mental benefit."

6. The Specifics of the Prophetic

To be prophetic is to speak the truth in situations with great integrity. Mentor Alex Mclean embodied this by sharing: "I had a prophetic word for a staff member at secondary school in Crawley. We would pray with the KICK staff based at the school. On the way to work in the car, I got a vision for the staff member who wasn't a Christian but had had experience of the Church before. They asked questions and knew we were a Christian organisation. I went to the morning prayer time and I wasn't sure about how to raise this with the Deputy Headteacher. I waited until the end of the day when we reported to him, and at the end of the debrief, I offered to share and pray with him. I saw a vision of his grandma in the hospital and that God wanted to say that He cares about her and wants to heal her. He started nearly crying because at lunchtime after I'd already got the vision, he then got the call to say that his grandma was in the hospital. Bonkers. We were taken aback and couldn't believe it. We ended up praying for him and his grandma. He then reported back a week and a half later that his grandma had been healed and made a full recovery. He now sends worship songs to us daily. He asks us to pray for him. It was a crazy testimony of God's love and goodness. There is a ministry of reminder. The Israelites named places by stone to help them not forget what God does and how He does it. We can remember what He does and what He has done."

7. Outside of the Box Ideas

To have integrity, we must innovate and adapt provisions to meet needs that continue to change. Church Pastor and former KICK Coach Andrew Dowey outlines, "We started the Merland Rise KICK Academy in October 2012, which continues to flourish today. There were five volunteers at first, and there were six children. After two years, we wondered if there would be any growth. We prayed, decided to persevere and could never have imagined what happened next. A local who had been through a tough time offered to help. He was struggling to find purpose in his life. After several months, he chose to become a Christian and was baptised. His witness in the local area and his 'outside of the box' ideas meant we made key changes to the age group we served. In the following four years, the KICK Academy doubled in size to over forty young people. We had older young people developing their own leadership skills and running sessions for the younger ones, going on to start careers in youth work and sports. Then came March 2020 and the challenges of COVID lockdowns. We didn't know if the KICK Academy would recover and, if so, how. The Lord was faithful as He was in the beginning, and the message was the same: 'Just keep turning up.' The numbers of children, young people and families are now even greater than pre-COVID times. God has blessed the KICK Academy and many young people have received expressions of God's love. We have much to be grateful for and look forward to seeing more!"

8. The Journey of Faith

It is easy to get distracted, especially when working with young people. Still, we can risk missing opportunities for faith when we do. Founding Coach Tom Rutter highlights how distractions can get in the way of life's momentous moments, "Taking a group of young people from the first KICK Academy in Richmond to the London churches' Football Tournament is another example of God's provision for KICK. We had a hectic journey by tube, so we had to ensure we got off at the right stop up to Regent's Park. It was a great relief to even arrive at Baker Street and then enter the park for the tournament. The Holy Trinity Church Richmond KICK Academy had entered several teams into the youth division age groups. They equipped themselves well but got knocked out before the business end of the tournament. However, this day will always be remembered when I watched on from a distance, filled with awe and delight at seeing two lads make eternally significant decisions. Standing listening to Mark Bythe giving a great Gospel talk – I had to quietly 'shhh' one of our volunteer coaches (Alex), who wanted to evaluate and run through how well the two teams had performed that afternoon. I tapped him on the shoulder and said, 'Look over there...' It was a total delight to see two of the lads that we had brought to the tournament, both of whom had been there from the start with our work in Richmond, make professions of faith and respond to the Gospel talk invitation. Witnessing this momentous decision was such a special moment in their – and my own – experience with KICK and such an answer to our prayers over the years!" Pure, indescribable joy in that moment.

9. True Integrity is Values-Driven

Before Easter 2024, we had confirmation that a headteacher wanted to proceed with KICK. He said they looked at four different companies but chose to go with KICK because of three reasons: "What swayed it was KICK's breadth of different sport/dance disciplines that you offer, the commitment to a values-driven approach and the support you give to your staff, investing in their training." We get lots of things wrong at KICK but the desire to improve in every area does shine through. Much of this stems from the leadership of Jonny Wright as Director of Quality. Jonny recently said, "KICK needs to be all about quality but the thing that I think sets us apart is our heart. There is a love in this place. We love the young people, and this is what makes us different." This is the secret of KICK's success, inspired by our Christian mission to demonstrate God's love. This is what transforms young people. We do not do our work in isolation from God but are inspired by Him. This is an expression of our commitment to integrity and to being true to our Christian ethos and ACEII values.

Summary

Therefore, integrity is a core value of KICK because young people need certainty and clarity. Integrity is important to demonstrate that we are reliable and true to our word, honest and up-front with our motives, objectives and motivations. If we are integral, then we are more likely to win the trust of those we serve; they will engage with us because they trust us. We want young people to feel safe to open up to us and for our advice to make a positive impact in their lives. With integrity, parents, carers, schools, churches, other stakeholders, or partners we work with, will also trust KICK. From that position of integrity, we can make sure we share, when given permission, a message of Good News that there is a God who is the Way, the Truth, and the Life (John 14). We have seen new opportunities to speak in the corridors of power, challenge stereotypes of gender and disability and go to new regions to engage the most disadvantaged young people. We are grateful for the opportunity to complete good works designed in advance for us to deliver (Ephesians 2:10). In order to value integrity, we need to contemplate how we, as KICK, will best walk in obedience to God and His ways. Being authentic and integral in our decision making can provide greater confidence and clarity to young people in their own faith journeys.

JOE LOWTHER

Chapter 12
Integrity: Spiritual Application

If the purpose of life is to know God and follow Him, then the Biblical principle, "to walk in obedience to God's ways" is central to the concept of integrity. What does it mean to walk in obedience, and why is it important? Where does it crop up in scripture? What are the opposite outcomes of not walking in obedience? What is the impact on those who do walk in obedience? As we look at some of these areas, I hope the Holy Spirit brings insights to mind and that in your heart, you might be determined to walk with integrity in obedience towards Him.

1. The Call to Walk in Obedience

Let's start with the passages which use the phrase "to walk in obedience".

Psalm 128:1 says, "Blessed are all who fear the Lord, who walk in obedience to Him." God wants you to be blessed. It is His heart's desire that you be free and safe. To fear the Lord is the beginning of wisdom; to walk in obedience to Him is to know His blessing. May this motivate us as we consider this value of integrity as we walk in obedience.

In Deuteronomy 5:32–33 in the final week of his life, Moses urges the people of Israel, "So be careful to do what the Lord your God has commanded you; do not turn aside to the right or to the left. Walk in obedience to all that the Lord your God has commanded you, so that you may live and prosper and prolong your days in the land that you will possess." Here, we are to be careful to walk in obedience. It is easy to run and stumble, rush and give up, or drift away from what God has commanded us. There are many temptations to lure us off course. We must be purposeful and careful to keep on the course and not turn to the right or left. God wants you to prosper by walking in obedience – how can you choose Him today?

In Jeremiah 7:23, God says, "But I gave them this command: 'Obey Me, and I will be your God, and you will be My people. Walk in obedience to all I command you, that it may go well with you." God wants things to go well with us. This is not a prosperity Gospel that we have, as we can see this in the suffering of Jesus and in eleven of the twelve disciples who were said to be martyred for their belief in Jesus and His promise of eternal life. But God loves us and wants to lead us on paths that will lead us to prosper spiritually and receive eternal life. It is our responsibility to obey Him and know the security that He is our God. He wants to be your God. Let that reality wash over you in your worship and respond with a renewed commitment to walk in obedience to a faithful God.

Therefore, we can see that God wants us to walk in obedience through the Torah, the Writings and the Prophets. He wants to bless us, prosper us and be with us when we walk in obedience. He calls us to this. We will now look at another example – the first example that drew me to this concept – this time in the histories of 1 Kings 11.

The context to this passage is that in 1 Kings 9:4–5 God says, "As for you, if you walk before Me faithfully with integrity of heart and uprightness, as David your father did, and do all I command and observe My decrees and laws, I will establish your royal throne over Israel forever, as I promised David your father when I said, 'You shall never fail to have a successor on the throne of Israel.'" Here, God reminds King Solomon of His promise to King David that his line would have a long-lasting reign by walking in obedience. Sadly, the first line of kings after King Solomon fell away from God. This is where we arrive at 1 Kings 11:29–40, and we will read:

1 Kings 11:29–40, "About that time Jeroboam was going out of Jerusalem, and Ahijah the prophet of Shiloh met him on the way, wearing a new cloak. The two of them were alone out in the country, and Ahijah took hold of the new cloak he was wearing and tore it into twelve pieces. Then he said to Jeroboam, 'Take ten pieces for yourself, for this is what the Lord, the God of Israel, says: 'See, I am going to tear the kingdom out of Solomon's hand and give you ten tribes. But for the sake of my servant David and the city of Jerusalem, which I have chosen out of all the tribes of Israel, he will have one tribe. I will do this because they have forsaken Me and worshipped Ashtoreth, the goddess of the Sidonians, Chemosh, the god of the Moabites, and Molek, the god of the Ammonites, and have not walked in obedience to Me, nor done what is right in My eyes, nor kept My decrees and laws as David, Solomon's father, did. But I will not take the whole kingdom out of Solomon's hand; I have made him ruler all the days of his life for the sake of David, My servant, whom I chose and who obeyed My commands and decrees. I will take the kingdom from his son's hands

and give you ten tribes. I will give one tribe to his son so that David, my servant, may always have a lamp before Me in Jerusalem, the city where I chose to put My name. However, as for you, I will take you, and you will rule over all that your heart desires; you will be king over Israel. If you do whatever I command you and walk in obedience to Me and do what is right in My eyes by obeying My decrees and commands, as David My servant did, I will be with you. I will build you a dynasty as enduring as the one I built for David and will give Israel to you. I will humble David's descendants because of this, but not forever.' Solomon tried to kill Jeroboam, but Jeroboam fled to Egypt, to Shishak the king, and stayed there until Solomon's death."

So, God has called the kings to walk in obedience, but we see in verse thirty-three that they have walked away from obedience. King Solomon broke the first and second commandments in worshipping other gods, and likely all the others. God was patient but just. His punishment split the Israelite Kingdom between Solomon's two sons, one King Rehoboam, whom Solomon anointed who ended up with only two of the twelve tribes on his side, and King Jeroboam, who ended up with ten of the tribes, as God had warned would happen. Neither king walked in obedience, but in verse thirty-eight, God reminded them that He was still prepared to uphold His side of the bargain to build an enduring dynasty if they would only walk in obedience. God wants us to walk. Walking is defined as, "To move at a regular pace by lifting and setting down each foot in turn, never having both feet off the ground at once." Let's walk at a regular pace with Him, being consistent in our habits to read the Bible, pray and spend time in His presence with His people at church. Let's keep one foot grounded, serving Him in the world, and lift the other foot off the ground in expectation of a heavenly union with our Lord Jesus for eternity. To walk is secondly defined by the Oxford Dictionary as, "To guide, accompany, or escort (someone) on foot."[28] Let's approach the Father, as we follow the Son, guided by the Holy Spirit. Let's walk in obedience, following Him in all of His ways. We are called to walk in obedience, for our own good, by a heavenly God.

2. How to Walk in Obedience

There are critical warnings of what the Bible warns are symptoms of a spiritually corrupted mind, such as rejection of authority and rebellion towards God and His ways. Instead, there are three ways we can walk uprightly with integrity and in obedience to God.

2.1. Know the truth

God wants us to know Him and His truth. We see this in 2 Timothy 2:15, "Do your best to present yourself to God as one approved, a worker who does not need to be ashamed and who correctly handles the word of truth." God is patient with us but notice when He says to "do your best." We do not need to be the best but must try our best to know the truth. This can then drive our decisions as we walk in obedience.

2.2. Live the Truth

In Luke 11:28, Jesus replied, "Blessed rather are those who hear the word of God and obey it." Integrity matters to God, and we know from James 1:22 that we are not to "merely listen to the word, and so deceive yourselves. Do what it says." If our faith is without works, it is dead. We are to walk in obedience with the integrity of action. You can't walk with God if you are dead in faith.

In Colossians 3:15–17, Paul writes, "Let the peace of Christ rule in your hearts, since as members of one body you were called to peace. And be thankful. Let the message of Christ dwell among you richly as you teach and admonish one another with all wisdom through psalms, hymns and songs from the Spirit, singing to God with gratitude in your hearts. And whatever you do, whether in word or deed, do it all in the name of the Lord Jesus, giving thanks to God the Father through Him". We are in this together as a body and Christ can rule our hearts with His peace. We are, yes, to work hard but as Christians we are to allow Christ through the Holy Spirit to lead, teach and admonish (warn) you in the ways of obedience. In Matthew 28:20, Jesus taught the disciples to "obey everything I have commanded you. And surely, I am with you always, to the very end of the age." This is not a walk on your own; remember, you have company on this journey of integrity.

2.3. Share the Truth

Thirdly, we are to not just know the truth and live for ourselves but also to share the truth with others as we walk in obedience. In 1 Peter 3:15–16 it calls, "But in your hearts revere Christ as Lord. Always be prepared to give an answer to everyone who asks you to give the reason for the hope that you have. But do this with gentleness and respect, keeping a clear conscience, so that those who speak maliciously against your good behaviour in Christ may be ashamed of their slander." Always be prepared to share what God has revealed to you with others. We are to do this without pride or for our fame, but in following the behaviour of Christ and for His glory. The reason for this is found in 2 Corinthians 4:5, "For what we preach is not ourselves, but Jesus Christ as Lord, and ourselves as your servants for Jesus' sake." It is the example of Jesus, who gave up everything to become a servant. His example of sacrificial love and the rhythms of His walk in obedience to His Father, are a North Star for us to follow. Read all of the Bible cover to cover, seeing how God unfolds His truth. Keep reading the Gospels to see how Jesus walked. He was never out of step with His Father and, with the perfect timing, ascended to Heaven, allowing the Holy Spirit to enter God's rescue story for all who choose to walk with God.

3. The Impact of Walking in Obedience

3.1. The Impact on Us

To walk in obedience will change our lives. Incrementally, yes, but also transformationally. To follow the footsteps of the Lord Jesus is the narrow path. Instead of being led to spiritual death, we can walk forward to life and life to the full that Jesus offers. We know that the Holy Spirit grows the fruits of character within our lives as we walk in obedience to Him. Would you like to be more at peace, have more self-control and be more faithful to those around you today? Choose Him afresh and obey Him by faith, then see Him impact your life.

3.2. The Impact on Those Around Us

In the context of false teachers deceiving people for selfish gain, 2 John 1:6 says, "And this is love: that we walk in obedience to His commands. As you have heard from the beginning, His command is that you walk in love." In our interactions with those around us, let's love one another and quietly demonstrate our love for God by walking in obedience to Him. Consider today how you might practically help someone in need that God draws to your attention. Chose to obey by faith because you wish to and not because you have to; if you are able to sincerely ask God to help you, He will answer.

3.2. The Impact on the Nation

By walking in obedience to God, we can have a powerful impact on those around us. Don't just do this for yourself and those you like but also for those around you, some of whom you may not like! Even to those far and wide. In Zechariah 3:6–7, "The angel of the Lord gave this charge to Joshua: 'This is what the Lord Almighty says: 'If you will walk in obedience and keep My requirements, then you will govern My house and have charge of My courts, and I will give you a place among these standing here.'" This was a specific promise to Joshua, not to everyone. It may not be a promise to you or me, but it is a general rule that in walking in obedience to God, He will give you responsibility. The size of responsibility is specific for each person and is not important. Social or professional status has no traction in God's kingdom. What is important is how we walk in obedience with what we have, following God for the benefit of others and the communities and country we live in. Walk in obedience and look for ways in which God is leading you to impact your community and make Jesus known, however big or small.

Summary

Therefore, we move in Christian integrity best when we walk in obedience to and in harmony with God. So let's listen to Him when He calls us, step forward in these ways and trust that His desire is to bless. Next, let's walk in obedience by knowing the truth, living the truth and sharing God's truth with others. Finally, allow God to make an impact within us, those around us and our nation. God wants us to be people of integrity, willing to act from a foundation of knowing Him and with gratitude for how fortunate we are. Is the Holy Spirit bringing a new area in your life to mind in which He wants you to walk in obedience? Let's courageously resolve to follow Jesus' example of integrity for the Father's glory.

Conclusion: Vision for the Future

In conclusion, I trust that you have enjoyed the journey of a wild ride of calling and adventure and have marvelled at a glorious God. I have sought to share insights of faith and testimonies of hope and to celebrate God's generous provision. KICK's Story sets out to inspire those passionate about the next generation, who dare to believe in God, and desire to make a difference. We will conclude by looking to the future within these three pillars.

1. The Next Generation

We can clearly see that many young people express a sense of hopelessness – for example, one-third of sixteen to twenty-four-year-olds in the UK (31%) report evidenced depression or anxiety. According to the NHS, since Lockdown, "Rates of a probable mental disorder, rose from one in ten (10.1%) in 2017 to one in six (17.7%). Many young people are anxious, but they are also unhappy – one in five young people now self-harm according to UNICEF and concerningly, sixty percent of terrorism referrals to the police are for under twenty-year-olds. Whatever our views are on certain statistics and definitions, it is surely clear to all of us that many of our young people experience a sense of hopelessness. Without hope, they have fear. Without hope, they have anger. Without hope, they have despair. Therefore, we want to bring them a hope for the future. We want those young people to believe in themselves, to have a social hope for their communities and most importantly, we want them to know the eternal hope, available to all who believe, and God's offer of eternal life, starting now and eventually through to Heaven. But we also want them to have fun whilst they get there. We want them to have joy in the present and enjoy the journey there. At KICK, our Theory of Change or otherwise known as our model of approach, is that we believe that a transformed life means change on a personal, social and spiritual level. We want to see personal growth to maturity and ongoing transformation. We aspire for our young people to know a hope for future and a joy in the present.

2. Dare to Believe in God

Lewis Smedes writes, "Hope is to our spirits what oxygen is to our lungs. Lose hope, and you die. They might not bury you for a while, but without hope, you are dead inside. Hope is the energy of the soul."[29] Hope is important. We too need to be reminded of how ever bleak things can get, hope exists. Hope can inspire missional adventure. We can have hope because we know the end from the beginning. We are within the Bible narrative, not after it. We sit ahead of Jesus' return and the triumph of His victory. We can have a hope for the future because of the past examples, the present stories and the promises that give security going forward. Throughout Scripture, we are reminded to have hope in God. Daniel was freed from the Lion's Den, Elijah defeated the prophets of Baal, David bested Goliath, God freed the Israelites from four hundred years of Egyptian slavery, and, most importantly, Jesus won us salvation on the Cross, rescued us from our condition without hope.

God gives hope for the present today. Psalm 9:18 says, "But God will never forget the needy; the hope of the afflicted will never perish." Therefore, we can have hope for the future because God knows the future and those in need today. Hope is always forward-looking, and we can be inspired by hope for the future because of what God will do in the future. In Psalm 25:3 it says, "No one who hopes in You will ever be put to shame." So, we can have a hope in God that He will take care of our future. Whether you are exhausted, scared, shamed, battered or feel defeated – you can have hope to begin a missional adventure.

In a beautiful synergy with this reality of needing a hope for the future, we can know a joy in the present. Joy is an inner feeling compared to happiness as an outward expression. Joy endures hardship and trials and connects with meaning and purpose. A person pursues happiness but chooses joy. So, joy is despite circumstance. It is hard to be happy, but it is potent to be joyful.

To be joyful in the present, let's look at three ways God calls us to be radically transformed by this fruit of the Spirit. Joyfulness is a spiritual state; let's ask the Holy Spirit to move within us as we reflect on these opportunities. Deuteronomy 16:14 says, "Be joyful at your festival – you, your sons and daughters, your male and female servants, and the Levites, the foreigners, the fatherless and the widows who live in your towns." It is good to celebrate with others and include everyone, looking for opportunities to recognise others and celebrate. Romans 12:15–16 emphasises that we are to "Rejoice with those who rejoice; mourn with those who mourn. Live in harmony with one another. Do not be proud but be willing to associate." Be honest in your interactions with each other. To rejoice is to keep being joyful. Do it repeatedly. Psalm 16:11 outlines that God, "You make known to me the path of life" and goes on "You will fill me with joy in Your presence, with eternal pleasures at Your right hand." God can lead and guide. He can show His presence in the present and eternal pleasures as we walk with Him. He is the One who can fill us with joy as we engage in the mission of today and tomorrow.

I trust that the testimonies through KICK's Story have inspired you to believe that God can provide hope for the future and that we can know that for ourselves and which will provide a foundation for us to hope for others. Furthermore, I trust that this has demonstrated that God is also able to give us a joy in the present. As He is the real Joy Giver, His joy is a gift that takes us beyond today's happiness and into a resolute state regardless of circumstance. These two areas of hope and joy are a dynamic combination. Proverbs 10:28 says, "The hope of the righteous is joy..." God is a God who sees in and beyond time. He wants us to experience joy and hope combined. God can fill us with joy by His Holy Spirit, as we see in Romans 15:13, "May the God of hope fill you with all joy and peace as you trust in Him, so that you may overflow with hope by the power of the Holy Spirit." He is the God of all hope. God wants to fill you with all joy from this position of strength. There is no better example that expresses the hope that God gives us of eternal life and the deep joy that this brings than that of the Parable of the Hidden Treasure – Matthew 13:44, "The Kingdom of Heaven is like treasure hidden in a field. When a man found it, he hid it again, and then in his joy went and sold all he had and bought that field." We know the Lord Jesus and what He has done. May we know and see this more deeply. As in this parable, it is like we have won the lottery because of this reality – our sinful souls are counted free! We can know the riches of joy today because of the hope of what He has in store for us. Through God's revelation to humankind in the Bible, God constantly shares His desire to be Abba Father to us, His children, and offers us hope for the future and joy in the present. Let's reflect on this hope and joy today. We've won the lottery, and let's dare to believe in the reality that God wins and allow this to impact the heart of our choices, decisions and motivations for those we serve.

3. Desire to Make a Difference

Throughout this book, we have seen that our core values (ACEII) shape and impact our vision and execution of our work. So, firstly, defining a mission is essential in order to know the why, how and what of our plans. God is a Master Builder, and He demonstrated that to us by providing direction, connections and funding as we made our decisions.

Secondly, to be aspirational on behalf of young people has been a crucial launch value as we dared to dream, saw lockdown salvation and lit fires across the UK. The lessons from the story of God's calling of Moses inspired our aspirations for young people.

Thirdly, we explored stories of compassion motivated by the pain of a tragic stabbing, the poverty of family breakdown and the reality of suicide during COVID-19. To truly show compassion, we learnt that we are to love God with all our heart, soul and strength; and then, with our heart pointed in the right direction and inspired by the love of God, to love our neighbour as ourselves.

Fourthly, values-driven coaching, forty parables through street dance, and the joy of kids climbing over the walls to come to KICK Academies, demonstrated the importance of excellence. Learning to pray like kings and queens is a spiritual application of this value.

Fifthly, through valuing intentional relationships, we reflected on coaches who learnt Romanian to communicate, who built trust to listen to the deep-rooted hurt of self-harm; and on our chaplains who counselled and baptised young people. As with building the wall in Nehemiah, the reality is that God asks us all to join in His master plans to intentionally build together for one Kingdom.

Finally, we looked at integrity with some illustrations of how we include all the young people regardless of ability, by sharing the prophetic where appropriate, and encouraging them to be brave and to persevere in KICK Academies, even though they may initially feel lost, but then are able to develop further. The spiritual application of integrity is to walk in obedience, know the truth and live it out, being trustworthy people and giving glory to God.

Therefore, Mission, Aspiration, Compassion, Excellence, Intention and Integrity are essential for those who desire to make a difference in the lives of young people.

Much despair is shared in regard towards the decline of the church in the UK. However, it is by contrast important to note that according to Bellings[30] research, the Christian faith is growing twice as fast as the global population. For example, Pentecostalism has seen four hundred percent growth, particularly in the southern hemisphere, and today, there are 2.6 billion Christians worldwide, which is the size of the combined populations of the USA and Europe. Christianity is spreading, not receding. Young people in the UK need a hope for the future and a joy in the present. Let's desire for a vision to make a difference. We need to be more ambitious for their sake and be confident that God is actively at work in our world today. The time is now; the time is urgent; use your time to build your own story, in step with His Spirit, for the sake of young people and His glory. Blessed be His name!

JOE LOWTHER

Epilogue: The Way Forward

In light of our desire to bring hope for the future and joy in the present, coupled with our vision to reach a generation of young people within a generation of time, we need to have commitment and creativity in the way forward. Children and young people need a holistic, not just academic, approach to their recovery; they for example need an injection of support and optimism to steer attitudes to education and they also need safe spaces when students require pastoral care.

In addition, they need a social approach. Being outdoors, active and doing hobbies is vital for young people's mental health and social connection. Although technology can help them stay connected, they still need face-to-face support. Those from disadvantaged backgrounds who have experienced significant issues since the pandemic, such as increased domestic violence and need added support. To count as a genuinely holistic response to their hopelessness, young people also need a spiritual response which includes a strategic focus on making the church more inclusive of younger needs and aspirations; churches need to embrace a theological understanding of the priesthood of all believers, in order to facilitate a whole church approach. We need to go out to young people and welcome them back to church. We need to realise that we have Good News and something to say to young people on the issues that matter to them such as isolation, a lack of hope and the threat to the environment; and finally to positively foster hope, meaning and a sense of purpose born of our belief in them.

We are excited about the future at KICK. Led by the exceptional Matt King, we have faithful and astute trustees, with a hugely talented staff team who believe in the mission. We are proud to collaborate with various sports ministry UK partners such as Christians in Sport, Ambassadors in Football, Sports Chaplaincy UK, Salvation Army Sport and SU Sport to name a few. We commend all of them to you for their brilliant work and commitment to mission. We are proud to partner with many exceptional organisations committed to this next generation of young people. We have been fortunate to meet to pray regularly with the CEOs of Youth for Christ, Scripture Union, Youth with a Mission (YWAM), Message Trust, Urban Saints and Young Life. In addition to the spiritual significance of prayer, we have run joint conferences, encouraged our staff to work together and explored joint projects. We build one Kingdom, not many. God is speaking – Youth for Christ, Urban Saints, and YWAM have all felt a sense of the need to refocus efforts towards discipleship. God is always preparing His body for any change that is coming; He knows what is around the corner, we must listen to Him.

We have been encouraged by recent partnerships with Scripture Union and a new joint language around working together. The Church of England has announced that it wants to double its young people by 2030. There is a coordinated move by Alpha International to bring churches and ministries together to recognise two thousand years since Jesus' death and resurrection in 2033. These examples are an encouragement that, as C.S. Lewis put it, "Aslan is on the move" in the UK.

At KICK, we importantly want to develop new services, such as music or coding, to reach new groups of young people who are uninterested in sport. We are keen to grow our work at Christian festivals and cheer on those doing great work in this space with the provision of sport and dance ministry. We want to be an organisation that is recruiting ahead of the curve, building capacity for growth, repositioning and innovating provision for the sake of young people. We are delighted to work collaboratively with Bible Colleges across the UK. We look forward to training both church volunteers for KICK Academies and demystifying parallel church work for new church leaders.

We want to continue to prepare our coaches and develop our people for work at KICK. We also see that our investment in them today contributes to training for future church leaders of tomorrow. Carey Nieuwhof,[31] in her ten predictions for the church's future, said, "Churches that love their model more than the mission will die." KICK, too, must be agile to adapt to new models and approaches to meet the needs of young people, respond to intermediary markets and innovate for opportunities as we evolve. We must continue to be foundationally Gospel-focused in our work, with the character of Jesus being our model and being intentional in sharing His love with others.

The core message of hope has not changed in a millennia but the methods of communicating that must be relevant in the way they are communicated to each generation. KICK needs to be prepared to further engage more young people through intermediaries such as schools, churches, parents and partners. We need simple models of ministry that can make the Gospel understandable and edible for young people, life easier for volunteers and scalable expansion more possible across the UK. KICK also requires an intricate offer that is attractive to schools, exciting for staff to work at, and responsive to the multiplicity of needs of young people.

To transform young people's lives, with God's love, through sport and support, we must grow and adapt our approach. Our problem is that hopelessness in young people exists. Our solution remains, it is quite simply to reach young people where they are. What happens if we fail is too much to risk. We must seek all kinds of new ways to offer a hope for the future and a joy in the present.

References

[1] Mind. 2024. 'Facts and Figures About Young People and Mental Health.' [Online]. Available at: https://www.mind.org.uk/about-us/our-strategy/doing-more-for-young-people/facts-and-figures-about-young-people-and-mental-health/#:~:text=1%20in%206%20young%20people,1%20in%209%20in%202017.&text=Nearly%20one%2Dthird%20of%2016,five%20years%20earlier%20(26%25).

[2] UNICEF. 2021. https://www.unicef-irc.org/publications/pdf/Playing-The-Game-Main-Report.pdf

[3] Gov.UK. 'Community Life Survey 2021/22: Wellbeing and Loneliness.' *Department for Culture, Media and Sport.* [Online]. Available at: https://www.gov.uk/government/statistics/community-life-survey-202122/community-life-survey-202122-wellbeing-and-loneliness#:~:text=There%20were%20differences%20by%20age,25%2D34%20(9%25)

[4] Crossman, E. 2002. Mountain Rain. Authentic Media.

[5] Quotable Quotes. 2024. 'Smith Wigglesworth: Quotes.' [Online]. Available at: https://www.goodreads.com/quotes/621574-great-faith-is-the-product-of-great-fights-great-testimonies

[6] Meade, A. 2014. 'Everything You Need to Know About the Charity Fundraising Crisis.' *The Guardian.* [Online]. Available at: https://www.theguardian.com/voluntary-sector-network/2015/jul/10/everything-you-need-to-know-charity-fundraising-crisis

[7] D.L. Moody Center. 2024. The Quotable Moody. [Online]. Available at: https://moodycenter.org/the-quotable-moody-d-l-moody-quotes/#:~:text="If%20we%20make%20a%20full,in%20the%20life%20to%20come."

[8] Lincoln, A. 2013. in Lord Charnwood's Abrham Lincoln: The Biography

[9] Hill, A. 2023. 'Young People Ditching Ambitions Over UK Cost of Living Crisis, Research Finds.' *The Guardian*. [Online]. Available at: https://www.theguardian.com/society/2023/sep/19/young-people-ditching-ambitions-over-uk-cost-of-living-crisis-research-finds

[10] De Souza, D. R. 2020. https://assets.childrenscommissioner.gov.uk/wpuploads/2021/02/cco-building-back-better-slides.pdf

[11] Barton, R. H. 2013. Pursuing God's Will Together: Discernment Practise for Leadership Groups. Publisher: Intervarsity Press Books.

[12] Sheppard, M. 2024. 'Fatherlessness and Its Impact on Children in the UK.' *Mark Sheppard: Lifestyle Blogger*. [Online]. Available at: https://www.mark-sheppard.com/fatherlessness-and-its-impact-on-children-in-the-uk/#google_vignette

[13] Dr Jordan-Wolf, R. 2022 'Talking Jesus Report 2022: What People in the UK Think of Jesus, Christians and Evangelism.' Talking Jesus. [Online]. Available at: https://talkingjesus.org/research

[14] Longfield, A. 2023. Submission to the COVID-19 Inquiry. [Online]. Available at: https://thecommissiononyounglives.co.uk/wp-content/uploads/2023/10/Anne-Longfield-written-evidence-submitted-to-the-Covid-Public-Inquiry.pdf

[15] Murkett, K. 'Parents Should Share Blame for Plummeting School Attendance.' The Spectator. [Online]. Available at: https://www.spectator.co.uk/article/parents-should-share-blame-for-plummeting-school-attendance/

[16] Sheila, A. 2020. 'How Can I Love God with All My Heart, Soul, Mind and Strength?' *Crosswalk*. [Online]. Available at: https://www.crosswalk.com/faith/bible-study/how-can-i-love-god-with-all-my-heart-soul-mind-and-strength.html

[17] Press Release: PE is being Squeezed Out of the Curriculum Due to Academic Over-Testing of Children, Say Teachers. 2019. [Online]. Available at: https://www.probonoeconomics.com/news/press-release-pe-is-being-squeezed-out-of-the-curriculum-due-to-academic-over-testing-of-children-say-teachers

[18] Eyre, E. L. J.; Adeyemi, L. J.; Cook, K.; Noon, M.; Tallis, J. & Duncan, M. 2022. 'Barriers and Facilitators to Physical Activity and FMS in Children Living in Deprived Areas in the UK: Qualitative Study.' *National Library of Medicine: National Center for Biotechnology Information.* Vol. 19(3), p. 1717.

[19] Ofsted. 2019. 'Safeguarding Children and Young People in Education from Knife Crime.' *Lessons from London*. [Online]. Available at: https://assets.publishing.service.gov.uk/media/5f5a269fe90e07207ac98082/

Knife_crime_safeguarding_children_and_young_people.pdf

[20] McCartney, C. 2024. The Sunday School Movement in Britain: 1900–1939. Cambridge University Press.

[21] Hilborne, S. 2022. 'More than 1 Million Teenage Girls Fall Out of Love with Sport.' *Women in Sport.* [Online]. Available at: https://womeninsport.org/news/more-than-1-million-teenage-girls-fall-out-of-love-with-sport/

[22] Office of National Statistics. 2023. 'Community Life Survey 2021/22: Wellbeing and Loneliness.' *Department for Culture, Media and Sport.* [Online]. Available at: https://www.gov.uk/government/statistics/community-life-survey-202122/community-life-survey-202122-wellbeing-and-loneliness#:~:text=There%20were%20differences%20by%20age,25%2D34%20(9%25)

[23] Robson, C. 2023. 'Impact of Loneliness on Young People's Health.' *Worth-It.* [Online]. Available at: https://www.worthit.org.uk/blog/loneliness-mental-health#:~:text=Loneliness%20leads%20to%20social%20withdrawal,to%20seek%20out%20those%20interactions.

[24] Ofsted. 2019. 'Safeguarding Children and Young People in Education from Knife Crime.' *Lessons from London.* [Online]. Available at: https://assets.publishing.service.gov.uk/media/5f5a269fe90e07207ac98082/Knife_crime_safeguarding_children_and_young_people.pdf

[25] UK National Census. 2021. [Online]. Available at: https://www.ons.gov.uk/census

[26] Scripture Union. 2020. [Online]. Available at: https://content.scriptureunion.org.uk/95-campaign#:~:text=With%2095%25%20of%20under%2D18s,support%20you%20on%20that%20journey.

[27] BBC. 2023. 'Hundreds of Churches Will Have to Close, says Kirk.' BBC Scotland News. [Online]. Available at: https://www.bbc.co.uk/news/uk-scotland-65645891

[28] Oxford English Dictionary. 2024. https://www.oed.com/?tl=true

[29] Smedes, L. 2024. https://www.azquotes.com/quote/832388

[30] Bellings, A. 2023. 'The Changing Face of the Global Church.' *Undeceptions*. [Online]. Available at: https://undeceptions.com/articles/the-changing-face-of-the-global-church/

[31] Nieuwhof, C. 2018. 'Ten Predictions About the Future Church and Shifting Attendance Patterns.' *Organisational and Cultural Trends.* https://careynieuwhof.com/10-predictions-about-the-future-church-and-shifting-attendance-patterns/

Gov.UK. 2022. Research Review Series: PE. *Ofsted*. [Online]. Available at: https://www.gov.uk/government/publications/research-review-series-pe/research-review-series-pe

JOE LOWTHER

About the Author

Joe Lowther was born and brought up in London. He is proudly married to Laura and loves being a dad to his three boys: Theo (13), Seth (11) and Josh (8). He is a passionate Christian and is grateful to have been blessed by the teaching, love and faithfulness of his church, Christian Fellowship, in Richmond at Halford House. Inspired by a love for cinema, Joe studied Film and Television at university. After a brief spell at Sky Sports News, Joe worked for an enterprising charity called City Gateway in Tower Hamlets. The charity grew from five staff to two hundred and fifty at its peak, and Joe completed his teaching qualifications at South Bank University. He became the Principal of the Academy Free School that was created. This school achieved "outstanding" at Ofsted in 2014. Joe then became CEO of KICK with a mission to transform young people's lives, with God's love, through sport and support. KICK has grown from seven staff to ninety-two in the last nine years and has gone national. Joe completed an MSc in Voluntary Sector Management at Bayes Business School. Among other things, Joe is an avid football, rugby, cricket and tennis fan, supporting Manchester United. Joe loves all things sport, faith and young people related.

JOE LOWTHER

About the Organisation

KICK's mission is to transform young people's lives with God's love through sport and support. Originally named KICK London, we were initially founded in collaboration between an inspirational coach (Tom Rutter), a local church (Holy Trinity Richmond) and a National charity (British Youth for Christ). KICK London was granted Charitable Status in 2003, which was inspired by the vision for the sports ministry of Youth for Christ. In 2004, Tom was appointed to work full-time for KICK London by the Board of Trustees. He worked closely with the inspiration of Jon Burns, the ideas of Barry Mason and the support of Trevor Patterson and those at Holy Trinity Richmond. A weekend Football KICK Academy was established within the area in connection with the church and contracts to deliver sports coaching in local schools were secured. At the end of 2005, based on the success of the work in Richmond, a management team was developed to establish a KICK London presence in Croydon. From this point, KICK London grew steadily under the leadership of trustee Matt King and Operations Manager Mark Anderson, seeing the organisation move into multiple boroughs across London with an increase in both school provision and church-based KICK Academies.

In 2014, the Board of Trustees decided they wanted to accelerate the growth of KICK London and built a new infrastructure to do so, which saw our first CEO appointed, Joe Lowther. In 2015, when we launched our Street Dance provision to schools around London, the team doubled in size. In 2016 we updated and developed our mentoring provision to offer Solutions Focused

Mentoring for Schools. This saw our mentoring provision grow by four hundred percent in a single year. In 2017, we continued to grow as an organisation, by which point we had trebled in size in just three years to have the privilege of engaging with over seven thousand five hundred young people each week. In 2019, we launched our new Chaplaincy service, enabling us to support more young people, and completed a rebrand to become KICK, freeing us of geographical restraint. In 2020 we delivered vital mentoring sessions and sport lessons to key worker children in the height of COVID-19 during the national lockdown. Despite a challenging year, we then decided to move national as a response to the growth in need of young people across the UK. In 2021 we grew out of London to the West Midlands, East Midlands and the East of England. This supercharged our growth from ten thousand young per week to seventeen thousand. In 2022 we expanded into the North East and North West regions of England and added the new tier of Directors at leadership level. We invested time in 2023 to grow deeper in the six regions we were within growing to engage twenty-eight thousand five hundred young people. In 2024 we plan to grow into the South and South East of England as we continue our vision to reach a generation of young people within a generation of time by 2035.

About PublishU

PublishU is transforming the world of publishing.

PublishU has developed a new and unique approach to publishing books, offering a three-step guided journey to becoming a globally published author!

We enable hundreds of people a year to write their book within 100-days, publish their book in 100-days and launch their book over 100-days to impact tens of thousands of people worldwide.

The journey is transformative, one author said,

"I never thought I would be able to write a book, let alone in 100 days... now I'm asking myself what else have I told myself that can't be done that actually can?'"

To find out more visit
www.PublishU.com

JOE LOWTHER

KICK STORY

Printed in Great Britain
by Amazon